LAYERS OF LEARNING
YEAR FOUR • UNIT SEVEN

CIVIL WAR
NATIONAL PARKS
PLATE TECTONICS
POST IMPRESSIONISM

Published by HooDoo Publishing
United States of America
© 2017 Layers of Learning
(Grilled Cheese BTN Font) © Fontdiner - www.fontdiner.com
ISBN #978-1545402672

Units at a Glance: Topics For All Four Years of the Layers of Learning Program

1	History	Geography	Science	The Arts
1	Mesopotamia	Maps & Globes	Planets	Cave Paintings
2	Egypt	Map Keys	Stars	Egyptian Art
3	Europe	Global Grids	Earth & Moon	Crafts
4	Ancient Greece	Wonders	Satellites	Greek Art
5	Babylon	Mapping People	Humans in Space	Poetry
6	The Levant	Physical Earth	Laws of Motion	List Poems
7	Phoenicians	Oceans	Motion	Moral Stories
8	Assyrians	Deserts	Fluids	Rhythm
9	Persians	Arctic	Waves	Melody
10	Ancient China	Forests	Machines	Chinese Art
11	Early Japan	Mountains	States of Matter	Line & Shape
12	Arabia	Rivers & Lakes	Atoms	Color & Value
13	Ancient India	Grasslands	Elements	Texture & Form
14	Ancient Africa	Africa	Bonding	African Tales
15	First North Americans	North America	Salts	Creative Kids
16	Ancient South America	South America	Plants	South American Art
17	Celts	Europe	Flowering Plants	Jewelry
18	Roman Republic	Asia	Trees	Roman Art
19	Christianity	Australia & Oceania	Simple Plants	Instruments
20	Roman Empire	You Explore	Fungi	Composing Music

2	History	Geography	Science	The Arts
1	Byzantines	Turkey	Climate & Seasons	Byzantine Art
2	Barbarians	Ireland	Forecasting	Illumination
3	Islam	Arabian Peninsula	Clouds & Precipitation	Creative Kids
4	Vikings	Norway	Special Effects	Viking Art
5	Anglo Saxons	Britain	Wild Weather	King Arthur Tales
6	Charlemagne	France	Cells & DNA	Carolingian Art
7	Normans	Nigeria	Skeletons	Canterbury Tales
8	Feudal System	Germany	Muscles, Skin, Cardio	Gothic Art
9	Crusades	Balkans	Digestive & Senses	Religious Art
10	Burgundy, Venice, Spain	Switzerland	Nerves	Oil Paints
11	Wars of the Roses	Russia	Health	Minstrels & Plays
12	Eastern Europe	Hungary	Metals	Printmaking
13	African Kingdoms	Mali	Carbon Chemistry	Textiles
14	Asian Kingdoms	Southeast Asia	Non-metals	Vivid Language
15	Mongols	Caucasus	Gases	Fun With Poetry
16	Medieval China & Japan	China	Electricity	Asian Arts
17	Pacific Peoples	Micronesia	Circuits	Arts of the Islands
18	American Peoples	Canada	Technology	Indian Legends
19	The Renaissance	Italy	Magnetism	Renaissance Art I
20	Explorers	Caribbean Sea	Motors	Renaissance Art II

www.Layers-of-Learning.com

3	History	Geography	Science	The Arts
1	Age of Exploration	Argentina & Chile	Classification & Insects	Fairy Tales
2	The Ottoman Empire	Egypt & Libya	Reptiles & Amphibians	Poetry
3	Mogul Empire	Pakistan & Afghanistan	Fish	Mogul Arts
4	Reformation	Angola & Zambia	Birds	Reformation Art
5	Renaissance England	Tanzania & Kenya	Mammals & Primates	Shakespeare
6	Thirty Years' War	Spain	Sound	Baroque Music
7	The Dutch	Netherlands	Light & Optics	Baroque Art I
8	France	Indonesia	Bending Light	Baroque Art II
9	The Enlightenment	Korean Peninsula	Color	Art Journaling
10	Russia & Prussia	Central Asia	History of Science	Watercolors
11	Conquistadors	Baltic States	Igneous Rocks	Creative Kids
12	Settlers	Peru & Bolivia	Sedimentary Rocks	Native American Art
13	13 Colonies	Central America	Metamorphic Rocks	Settler Sayings
14	Slave Trade	Brazil	Gems & Minerals	Colonial Art
15	The South Pacific	Australasia	Fossils	Principles of Art
16	The British in India	India	Chemical Reactions	Classical Music
17	The Boston Tea Party	Japan	Reversible Reactions	Folk Music
18	Founding Fathers	Iran	Compounds & Solutions	Rococo
19	Declaring Independence	Samoa & Tonga	Oxidation & Reduction	Creative Crafts I
20	The American Revolution	South Africa	Acids & Bases	Creative Crafts II

4	History	Geography	Science	The Arts
1	American Government	USA	Heat & Temperature	Patriotic Music
2	Expanding Nation	Pacific States	Motors & Engines	Tall Tales
3	Industrial Revolution	U.S. Landscapes	Energy	Romantic Art I
4	Revolutions	Mountain West States	Energy Sources	Romantic Art II
5	Africa	U.S. Political Maps	Energy Conversion	Impressionism I
6	The West	Southwest States	Earth Structure	Impressionism II
7	Civil War	National Parks	Plate Tectonics	Post Impressionism
8	World War I	Plains States	Earthquakes	Expressionism
9	Totalitarianism	U.S. Economics	Volcanoes	Abstract Art
10	Great Depression	Heartland States	Mountain Building	Kinds of Art
11	World War II	Symbols & Landmarks	Chemistry of Air & Water	War Art
12	Modern East Asia	The South	Food Chemistry	Modern Art
13	India's Independence	People of America	Industry	Pop Art
14	Israel	Appalachian States	Chemistry of Farming	Modern Music
15	Cold War	U.S. Territories	Chemistry of Medicine	Free Verse
16	Vietnam War	Atlantic States	Food Chains	Photography
17	Latin America	New England States	Animal Groups	Latin American Art
18	Civil Rights	Home State Study I	Instincts	Theater & Film
19	Technology	Home State Study II	Habitats	Architecture
20	Terrorism	America in Review	Conservation	Creative Kids

Unit 4-7 Printable Pack

This unit includes printables at the end. To make life easier for you we also created digital printable packs for each unit. To retrieve your printable pack for Unit 4-7, please visit

www.layers-of-learning.com/digital-printable-packs/

Put the printable pack in your shopping cart and use this coupon code:

414UNIT4-7

Your printable pack will be free.

Layers of Learning Introduction

This is part of a series of units in the Layers of Learning homeschool curriculum, including the subjects of history, geography, science, and the arts. Children from 1st through 12th can participate in the same curriculum at the same time - family school style.

The units are intended to be used in order as the basis of a complete curriculum (once you add in a systematic math, reading, and writing program). You begin with Year 1 Unit 1 no matter what ages your children are. Spend about 2 weeks on each unit. You pick and choose the activities within the unit that appeal to you and read the books from the book list that are available to you or find others on the same topic from your library. We highly recommend that you use the timeline in every history section as the backbone. Then flesh out your learning with reading and activities that highlight the topics you think are the most important.

Alternatively, you can use the units as activity ideas to supplement another curriculum in any order you wish. You can still use them with all ages of children at the same time.

When you've finished with Year One, move on to Year Two, Year Three, and Year Four. Then begin again with Year One and work your way through the years again. Now your children will be older, reading more involved books, and writing more in depth. When you have completed the sequence for the second time, you start again on it for the third and final time. If your student began with Layers of Learning in 1st grade and stayed with it all the way through she would go through the four year rotation three times, firmly cementing the information in her mind in ever increasing depth. At each level you should expect increasing amounts of outside reading and writing. High schoolers in particular should be reading extensively, and if possible, participating in discussion groups.

These icons will guide you in spotting activities and books that are appropriate for the age of child you are working with. But if you think an activity is too juvenile or too difficult for your kids, adjust accordingly. The icons are not there as rules, just guides.

😊 1st-4th
😊 5th-8th
😊 9th-12th

Within each unit we share:

EXPLORATIONS, activities relating to the topic;
EXPERIMENTS, usually associated with science topics;
EXPEDITIONS, field trips;
EXPLANATIONS, teacher helps or educational philosophies.

In the sidebars we also include Additional Layers, Famous Folks, Fabulous Facts, On the Web, and other extra related topics that can take you off on tangents, exploring the world and your interests with a bit more freedom. The curriculum will always be there to pull you back on track when you're ready.

www.layers-of-learning.com

UNIT SEVEN

CIVIL WAR - NATIONAL PARKS - PLATE TECTONICS - POST-IMPRESSIONISM

Most folks are as happy as they make up their minds to be.
-Abraham Lincoln

LIBRARY LIST

HISTORY	Search for: Underground Railroad, Harriet Tubman, Civil War, Robert E. Lee, Abraham Lincoln, Reconstruction
	😊 Sweet Clara and the Freedom Quilt by Deborah Hopkinson. Based on a true story.
	😊 Follow the Drinking Gourd by Jeanette Winter.
	😊 I Am Abraham Lincoln by Brad Meltzer.
	😊 Abe Lincoln: The Boy Who Loved Books by Kay Winters.
	😊 😊 DK Eyewitness: Civil War by DK.
	😊 😊 Abraham Lincoln by Ingri and Edgar d'Aulaire.
	😊 The Price of Freedom: How One Town Stood Up To Slavery by Dennis and Judith Fradin. A fictionalized account of a true story.
	😊 Fields of Fury: The American Civil War by James McPherson. A non-fiction account of the Civil War by one of the foremost historians on the topic.
	😊 Across Five Aprils by Irene Hunt.
	😊 Like A River: A Civil War Novel by Kathy Cannon Wiechman.
	😊 The Civil War: An Interactive History Adventure by Matt Doeden.
	😊 Secrets of a Civil War Submarine: Solving the Mysteries of the H.L. Hunley by Sally M. Walker. Fascinating text and gorgeous pictures.
	😊 Shades of Gray by Carolyn Reeder. The story of a young boy, orphaned by the Civil War, and the struggle to create a life again in the aftermath.
	😊 😊 Abraham Lincoln's World by Genevieve Foster. Takes a cross cut of the history of the world at the time Abraham Lincoln was alive. Highly recommended.
	😊 😊 Harriet Tubman: Conductor on the Underground Railroad by Ann Petry.
	😊 😊 The Red Badge of Courage by Stephen Crane.
	😊 😊 Lincoln: A Photobiography by Russell Freedman. This book is excellent.
	😊 Underground Railroad: Authentic Narratives and Fist-Hand Accounts by William Still.
	😊 Uncle Tom's Cabin by Harriett Beecher Stowe.
	😊 Little Women by Louisa May Alcott.
	😊 Gods and Generals by Michael Shaara. First in a fictional trilogy about the Civil War based on the Battle of Gettysburg.
	😊 Battle Cry of Freedom by James McPherson. This is considered the definitive single volume book on the Civil War. Well-written and entertaining book.
	😊 A Short History of Reconstruction by Eric Foner. Excellent analysis of the reasons behind some of the problems Americans are still facing today.

GEOGRAPHY	Search for: National Parks, Yellowstone, Yosemite, John Muir, Theodore Roosevelt 😊 John Muir: America's Naturalist by Thomas Locker. 😊 The Camping Trip That Changed America by Barb Rosenstock. 😊 😊 Junior Ranger Activity Book by National Geographic Kids. 😊 John Muir: America's First Environmentalist by Kathryn Lasky. 😊 😊 John Muir: My Life With Nature by Joseph Cornell. 😊 😊 The National Parks: America's Best Idea by Ken Burns and Dayton Duncan. This is both a documentary movie and a companion book. Both are well worth your time.
SCIENCE	Search for: plate tectonics. This is a hard-to-find topic; look in more general books about earth science for specific sections on the topic. 😊 😊 Why Do Volcanoes Erupt? by Prodigy Wizard. 😊 What is the Theory of Plate Tectonics? by Craig Saunders. 😊 Alfred Wegener: Uncovering Plate Tectonics by Greg Young. 😊 😊 Plate Tectonics: The Engine Inside the Earth by Judith Hubbard. Good explanations in easy to understand language.
THE ARTS	Search for: Post-Impressionism, Neo-Impressionism, Van Gogh, Seurat, Gauguin, Cézanne. 😊 😊 Paul Gauguin by Mike Venezia. This book is from the Getting to Know the World's Greatest Artists series. 😊 😊 Georges Seurat by Mike Venezia. This is another one from the Getting to Know the World's Greatest Artists series. 😊 😊 The Yellow House by Susan Goldman Rubin. This is about two friends, Vincent Van Gogh and Paul Gauguin, living and painting together in France. This is their story, infused with several of their paintings. 😊 😊 Van Gogh and the Post-Impressionists For Kids: Their Lives and Ideas, 21 Activities by Carol Sabbeth. This book combines activities with a lot more information about the art and artists of this era. 😊 😊 😊 Post-Impressionism by Colin Wiggins. Part of the Eyewitness Art series. It has lots of illustrations with descriptions and information about all kinds of topics surrounding Post-Impressionism. A great reference for people of all ages. 😊 😊 😊 Van Gogh and Friends Art Game by Wenda O'Reilly. Learn about Post-Impressionists as you play a Go Fish style game.

HISTORY: CIVIL WAR

At the Constitutional Convention in 1787 George Mason, a Virginia slave owner and Founding Father said, "Every master of slaves is born a petty tyrant. [Slaves] bring the judgment of heaven on a Country. As nations can not be rewarded or punished in the next world they must be in this. By an inevitable chain of causes & effects Providence punishes national sins, by national calamities." The South had encouraged and protected, with violence when necessary, the bloody institution of slavery, and the North had let them get away with it and contributed to it through the slave trade. Ultimately between 618,000 to 750,000 people died eradicating slavery from North America.

This is a depiction of the Battle of Gettysburg, made famous because of the huge loss of life as well as the famous speech by Lincoln. Between 46 and 51 thousand casualties from both sides occurred during this three day battle, which is still the most costly of any battle in United States history.

The slavery issue had been on the table for a very long time, but several events made the issue break out in war. Congress had been trying to sidestep the issue, not having enough votes to either eradicate slavery or to make it a permanent institution. They tried compromise after compromise, which really made neither side happy. Congress also made contradictory laws, and the Supreme Court contradictory decisions, as first one side then other gained ascendancy. More and more people became convinced that slavery could not be solved by the law.

Then there were several violent events that renewed national interest in the question including the John Brown attack, the Bloody Kansas events, and the murderous attack on the senate

Fabulous Fact

While there was more to the Civil War than just slavery, it was this one issue that caused the war.

The Southern states fought for states' rights to keep slaves. The economy of the South was agrarian because of the slave culture. The Southern states seceded in order to keep slavery.

Additional Layer

To understand why the North wanted union badly enough to go to war, watch this alternate history for insight: https://www.youtube.com/watch?v=yhNbgoeEU-wM

Deep Thoughts

Why did southerners fight so hard to keep slavery?

Slavery was about money. The entire economy and way of life in the South was based on slavery. Even if you didn't own slaves yourself, your livelihood was based on that economy. Southerners weren't necessarily more evil than northerners, but they did have much more at stake if they chose equality.

floor of anti-slavery Charles Sumner by the pro-slavery Preston Brooks, an attack which left Sumner bedridden for more than two years while he recovered. (Sumner's first speech upon returning to the Senate was an anti-slavery one.)

The abolitionists were gaining ground and emerging from the fringes to mainstream politics. They founded a political party in 1854 specifically to oppose slavery, but also to promote the ideals of freedom and limited government espoused by Thomas Jefferson. They named it the Republican Party. Their first successful candidate was Abraham Lincoln, considered a moderate since he promised to not interfere with current slavery, but only to stop its spread. In that same election the anti-slave forces took control of the House and Senate. To the South it was obvious that their "peculiar institution" was about to end legislatively, so they preemptively decided to secede before Lincoln took office.

The South had been talking secession for awhile, and it was this issue that split the Democrat party in the 1860 election into northern and southern factions. All Democrats were agreed in their support of slavery and refusal to view black people as fully human, but the northern Democrats disagreed over whether secession was the solution. Even if the Democrats had remained united, the 1860 election would have been won by Lincoln and the House and Senate by the Republicans. Slavery was on the way out.

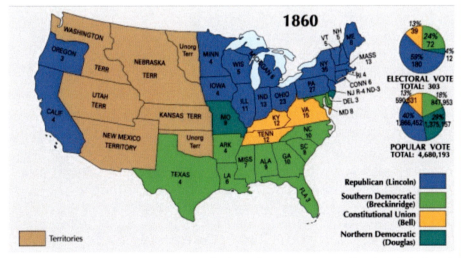

The southern states seceded early in 1861 and seized federal government buildings and military depots in the South. Lincoln moved to resupply the federal depot at Fort Sumter in April of 1861, first warning the Confederacy that he was on the way in an effort to avoid bloodshed. But the fort opened fire on the unarmed merchant ship bearing the supplies, and the war was officially begun. The conflict dragged on through five horrific years.

Famous Folks

Henry Clay was an influential politician from Tennessee from the time of James Madison and the War of 1812 until the 1850s.

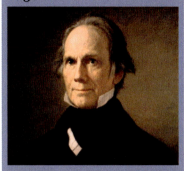

Though born into a wealthy slave-owning family, Clay believed in ending slavery. He fought to keep the nation together through the strife over slavery and was instrumental in the Compromise of 1850, an attempt to head off Civil War. Clay is considered one of America's most influential senators.

Additional Layer

The Civil War was on the horizon for decades before it actually broke out. The Compromise of 1850 was one of the measures that staved off war for a time.

Read more about it: http://history1800s. about.com/od/slavery- inamerica/a/compro- mise-of-1850.htm

Famous Folks

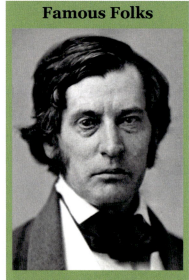

Charles Sumner was a senator from Massachusetts. He fought hard throughout his career to destroy slavery. Once the Civil War broke out he tried to beat the South and keep foreign nations from recognizing the Confederate government. After the war he was the leader of the Radical Republican faction in the government and worked tirelessly to ensure voting and other civil rights to the newly freed slaves, fighting against both Andrew Johnson and the Southern Democrats.

On the Web

There were several events that helped to raise emotions in the United States and trigger the Civil War.

http://www.civilwar.org/education/history/civil-war-overview/triggerevents.html

☺ ☺ ☺ EXPLORATION: Timeline

This timeline is a very short version of the Civil War, with only a couple of battles. You may want to create an extra "pop-out" timeline for just the Civil War years with your older kids. Printable timeline squares are at the end of this unit.

- 1820 Missouri Compromise admits one free state for every slave state admitted to keep the balance of political power
- 1850 Compromise of 1850 made the new territory of California a free state and allowed all other new states and territories to decide for themselves
- 1850 Fugitive Slave Act made it a crime to aid and abet runway slaves; free blacks are kidnapped and carried South
- 1857 Supreme Court rules against Dred Scott who sued for his freedom; he was ruled to be "property"
- Oct 1859 John Brown attempts to start a slave revolt by attacking the federal arsenal at Harper's Ferry, Virginia.
- Nov 6, 1860 Abraham Lincoln elected president
- Jan 1861 The South secedes
- April 1861 Attack on Fort Sumter
- July 1861 First Battle of Bull Run
- May 1862 "Stonewall" Jackson defeats the North at Shenandoah Valley, almost making it to Washington D.C.
- Jan 1863 Emancipation Proclamation goes into effect
- May 1863 Vicksburg Campaign by Ulysses S. Grant, Union win
- June-July 1863 Battle of Gettysburg
- Feb 1865 Sherman's March
- April 1865 Surrender at Appomattox Courthouse
- April 1865 Lincoln is assassinated

☺ ☺ EXPLORATION: The Underground Railroad

The Underground Railroad was a network of free blacks and whites in the north who hid, fed, cared for, and transported escaping slaves. After the Fugitive Slave Act of 1850, fleeing slaves had to be transported clear to Canada. Some also fled to Mexico, Florida, the West, and the Caribbean.

If you were a person who helped or hid escaping slaves you probably only knew three or four other contacts in your area who would let you know if a slave or group of slaves was on the way. They would secretly come to your house in the dead of night, concealed in the false bottom of a wagon or in disguise. You would feed them and give them a place to sleep for a day or two, and then you would figure out how to transport them secretly to the next station. You never knew where they came from or where they went. You were breaking the law just by helping them and could be fined or imprisoned (or if you were black, sold into slavery). One did not become a part of the Underground Railroad lightly.

Learn the language of the Underground Railroad, the words used to conceal the real meanings, words you could mutter in the street or outside the church to one you knew was part of the network.

- Gospel Train or Freedom Train: Underground Railroad
- Preachers: leaders and spokespersons for the Underground Railroad
- Agent: someone who coordinated escape routes and made contacts
- Conductor: person who transported slaves
- Baggage: escaping slaves in the network
- Shepherds: people who escorted escaping slaves
- Station Master: keeper or owner of a safe house
- Station: safe house
- Promised Land or Canaan or Heaven: Canada
- River Jordan: Ohio River
- Drinking Gourd: Big Dipper constellation, used to navigate northward
- Wind blows from the south: a slave hunter is in the area

Make a 3-D map of two stations on the Underground Railroad and the route between them. Start with a piece of cardboard as your base. Paint it to show rivers, roads, farm land, and forests. Then add some 3-D paper structures to show your stations. There is a printable of Underground Railroad figures at the end of this

Additional Layer

The Fugitive Slave Act of 1850 required that all escaped slaves must be returned to their masters and compelled officials and citizens to aid in the return of these slaves. Abolitionists called it the "bloodhound law." It meant that anyone caught aiding escaped slaves could be sent to jail or, if you were black, you could be kidnapped and sent to slavery. From this time escaping slaves had to leave the United States to be truly free, a sad irony.

Fabulous Facts

Escaping slaves and their helpers developed various codes, passwords and signs so they would be able to identify help along the way. The codes were very secret and not shared lightly. They were never written down, so there were probably many methods we know nothing of. For the rest we have to make some guesses. Lanterns, code words, and songs may all have been used. But usually the people along the network personally knew others who they could pass the fleeing slaves along to.

Famous Folks

Harriett Tubman was born a slave in Maryland. Never very submissive, she escaped as a young woman using the aid of the Underground Railroad. She returned 13 times, risking her own freedom, to aid others to be free as well. She used the song "Go Down Moses" to signal slaves to be ready or to hide. Besides her work on the Underground Railroad she became an active abolitionist and was nicknamed "Moses" by William Lloyd Garrison. During the Civil War she was an army scout and led armed raids, the only woman to do so. After the war she helped freedmen establish new lives and worked for women's rights. Take the time to read her story in depth.

unit. The woman with the rifle is Harriet Tubman. Label the map with some of the Underground Railroad words from above.

☺ ☺ ☺ **EXPLORATION: Map of the United States 1861**
Here's what the U.S. looked like on the eve of the Civil War.

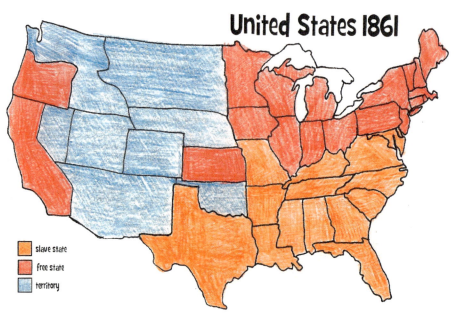

United States 1861

slave state
free state
territory

Kansas was admitted as a free state in January of 1861, and the Colorado territory was formed out of western Kansas and eastern Utah territories. The states of Delaware, Maryland, Kentucky, and Missouri were slave states, but they refused to secede so they were part of the Union during the Civil War. Many books call them "border states." West Virginia is still part of Virginia on this map; it will split off in 1863 over the secession issue and become a "border state" in the Union. Color the map from the end of this unit to show the slave states, free states, and territories on the eve of the Civil War. You can have your kids write in the names of the states that are shown for extra practice.

☺ ☺ **EXPLORATION: States' Rights and the 10th**
Back in the pre-Civil War days everybody was yelling "States' Rights! States' Rights!" What were they talking about?

They were talking about the Tenth Amendment, which says:

The powers not delegated to the United States by the Constitution, nor prohibited by it to the States are reserved to the States respectively, or to the people.

First, print the Tenth Amendment from the end of this unit. Then cut apart the amendment into phrases or words, depending on the ages of your children. Have your kids glue the words on to a poster board in the right order, giving them prompts and hints as needed.

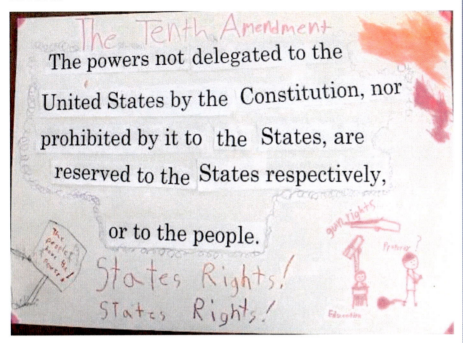

Next, discuss the meaning of the amendment with your kids. Basically the amendment means that the Constitution gives certain enumerated, or exactly spelled out, powers to the federal government, and everything else is the province of the states or the people. It means, federal government, back off!

During the years running up to the Civil War there were many attempts to outlaw slavery through the legislative branch or the judicial branch. The Southern states said the federal government didn't have the right to make laws regarding slavery because that was not specifically enumerated in the Constitution.

What do you think of that argument and do you think it applied to slavery? Why or why not? What role did the Declaration of Independence and its principles have in this debate?

Finally, draw pictures or write words on the poster that relate to the amendment.

☺ ☺ ☺ EXPLORATION: Abraham Lincoln

Abraham Lincoln was born in 1809 in a one room log cabin in Kentucky. As a frontier boy he had to do a lot of hard work, but he didn't like it much, and so he worked even harder to become educated by reading every book he could get his hands on. Eventually he passed the bar exam and began practicing law. He also

Fabulous Fact

Congress decided that Kansas voters would be the ones to decide if Kansas would enter the Union as a free state or a slave state. The future of slavery itself was at stake since Kansas would tip the legislative votes in Congress toward either free or slave. This meant that each side tried to gain the upper hand in Kansas. Non-Kansans moved into the state to influence the vote. It turned violent with murder, armed conflicts, arson, property destruction, and even an attack on the Senate floor.

The violence highlighted the lengths to which people would go to abolish or retain slavery and suggested that in the end armed conflict would be the only way.

Teaching Tip

Discuss what people mean and what they want in today's political environment when they speak about states' rights.

This will help your kids to understand why history is important, to see connections to human nature, and to analyze their own world more clearly.

ran for office at nearly every level of government and at every opportunity. He lost far more often than he won, but he gained a reputation for giving great speeches and following through with his promises. If Abe Lincoln told you he believed it, he really did.

By 1846, when he was elected to Congress, Lincoln was speaking out against injustices such as the Mexican-American War and slavery. After the Dred Scott Decision stripped slaves of all human rights, Lincoln spoke out vehemently. His famous "House Divided" speech was given at this time.

Have your high school student watch historian Matthew Pinsker read and explain the speech: https://www.youtube.com/watch?v=fcAGJzj2FSw

Watch this short biography about Lincoln with your younger kids: https://www.youtube.com/watch?v=L80_q2tPveo

Read more about Abraham Lincoln in books from the library or in resources you find online. As you read look for a quote or principle of Lincoln's that you think is important.

Make a puppet of Lincoln, using the template from the end of this unit. You may want to print it on card stock or glue it to thin cardboard so it is stiff. The puppet's arms and legs should be attached with brads so they can move. Then tie a string from the head and hands of the puppet to a stick. Move the stick to make your puppet's hands move. On the back of the puppet write the quote or principle you found in your reading. Have your puppet Lincoln explain the quote, what it means, and what it has to do with the Civil War or government.

☺ ☺ ☺ EXPLORATION: Civil War Soldier

Most Civil War soldiers were away from their families for the duration of the war years. Northern soldiers were fairly well supplied with uniforms, haversacks, tents, and food rations, but southern soldiers were lacking even these essentials, often having to live off the land and raid farms to eat, especially as the war wore on. The southerners also liberated whatever northern army equipment they could, especially favoring the waterproof blankets and tents of the North. None of the soldiers really ate well. In the North they had hardtack and old meat. In the South the soldiers ate cornbread and, if they were lucky, meat provided by the army, but more often if there was meat it was a squirrel or possum they caught themselves. They endured blistering heat and freezing cold. The soldiers were often sick and more died of disease than died in battle.

Read some of these accounts from people who lived during the Civil War: http://www.gacivilwar.org/stories

Civil War soldiers missed their families a great deal and wrote lots of letters home. They eagerly awaited the mail, and if it were late they were very put out.

After you have read some accounts above and learned some background about the Civil War, write a letter as though it is 1862. You can pretend to be a soldier or you could be someone back home writing to a soldier. Be sure to include as many details as you can.

☺ ☺ ☺ EXPLORATION: Civil War Animals
Pets were strictly forbidden in the camps and so, of course, many of the men had them. Dogs were the most popular, but cats, raccoons, chipmunks, and other wild animals were also kept. The cavalry officers had their horses, and many of those became beloved pets as well.

A few of these animals became mascots for their regiments. Read the accounts of some beloved animals at the City of Alexandria's website: https://www.alexandriava.gov/historic/fortward/default.aspx?id=40198

Have your older kids read this account of Civil War horses: http://ushistoryscene.com/article/civilwaranimals/

Choose one of the famous Civil War animals you read about and draw a picture of it. You can find a how-to-draw tutorial online for just about any animal. After you draw the animal, write some facts about it as related to the Civil War on your drawing. Tell about the animal in front of an audience.

☺ ☺ EXPLORATION: Gettysburg
In spite of being outnumbered and out-supplied, the South was winning most of the battles of the Civil War. Their biggest strength was their brilliant and inspiring general, Robert E. Lee. In the spring of 1863 Lee decided that on the tails of several southern victories he would march his armies north and invade Pennsylva-

Additional Layer
An eagle named Old Abe was the most famous of all the Civil War animal mascots.

Famous Folks
Dred Scott was a slave who sued for his freedom after his master took him to live in a free state for several years. The Supreme Court ruled that no black person could be a citizen and could not therefore bring a lawsuit in the United States.

Memorization Station
Learn about the Gettysburg Address by watching this video: http://goo.gl/I21Aej

Then memorize the speech: http://avalon.law.yale.edu/19th_century/gettyb.asp

When memorizing, write the speech up on a chalkboard or wall, repeating it over and over, in chunks together. Erase words here and there as you go until you've got it all.

Use the puppet when you recite it.

On the Web

You can make a timeline of Lincoln's life on a stovepipe hat printable here: http://www.layers-of-learning.com/abraham-lincoln-timeline/

On the Web

Watch this Crash Course video on the Civil War: https://www.youtube.com/watch?v=rY9zH-NOjGrs, then watch part 2, which is even better.

Additional Layer

The Civil War changed the entire nature of the government. The federal government grew enormous in power compared to states.

That trend toward federal power has continued ever since.

Civil War aside, do you think the change was good or bad? Explain.

nia in the hopes that this would frighten the war-weary northern politicians into suing for peace. It would also draw the war away from ravaged Virginia, giving it a rest.

The North and South met at a little town called Gettysburg and fought for three brutal days. But in the end it was the South that was defeated with huge losses. Lee retreated back to Virginia, the resolve of the North hardened, and all hope of foreign help for the South ended with the defeat. Many historians consider the Battle of Gettysburg the turning point of the war, the point from which the South began to lose consistently.

Watch this (click on the animated map): http://www.civilwar.org/battlefields/gettysburg/maps/gettysburg-animated-map/

After you have watched, discuss what you have seen.

- How important was strategy to Civil War battles? What were some of the Northern strategies that helped them win this battle? What were some of the mistakes in strategy on both sides?
- During the battle General Lee was "blind" to the Northern troop movements because of terrain and poor reconnaissance. With good information do you think the battle would have gone differently? How would a Southern win have affected the rest of the war?
- What weapons did the men use in this battle? How are they alike and different from modern military weapons?
- The battle had enormous numbers of casualties. What effect do you think this had on the men during the battle and just afterward?
- What effect do you think the battle had on the civilians who lived in the area? (See the sidebar on the previous page with an eyewitness account from a teenage girl.)

Draw your own map of the battle using a battle map from the internet as a guide. After you've made the map, cut flaps in it with a craft knife. Inside each flap put facts about the battle. You could include the generals, Pickett's charge, numbers of wounded and killed, weapons used, or information about the aftermath.

☺ ☻ EXPLORATION: Clara Barton

Clara Barton is most famous for her role in serving the wounded men of the Civil War. For more than a year she begged the Army and government officials to allow her to set up nursing stations and hospitals near the front lines of the war to aid the wounded and sick men. Finally she got her wish and began a nursing corps, working right on the battlefields. In 1864 she was officially named the "lady in charge" of the Army hospitals. The men called her the angel of the battlefield.

After the war she set up an "Office of Missing Soldiers." She and her assistants found and properly buried more than 55,000 missing soldiers.

A few years later she took a tour of Europe where she learned about the Red Cross. She brought the idea back to America and fought to get a Red Cross established in the United States. It took eight years of hard work, but she made it happen. The mission of the American Red Cross to this day is to assist soldiers and their families and to aid in natural disasters.

Read more about Clara Barton, and then make a paper nurse's hat. You'll need a piece of white printer paper, red paper or paint, a hole punch, and yarn.

1. Fold the piece of paper in half lengthwise. Position the fold on the side furthest from you.
2. Make a mark 3/4 of an inch from the fold and fold the paper again, creasing all the way across.
3. Turn the paper over so the new fold is on the bottom. Fold the corners up (opposite from the narrow fold) into a triangle on each side. Turn the paper over again.
4. The narrow fold becomes the band of the hat. Punch a hole in each end and thread a piece of yarn through. You will use this to tie the hat on.
5. Make a red cross on the hat with red paper or paint.

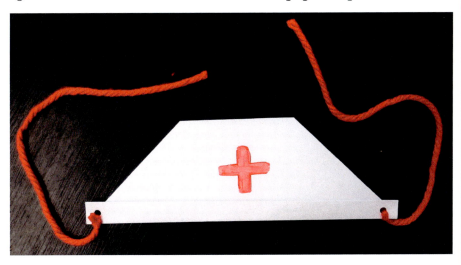

😊 😊 😊 **EXPLORATION: Ironclads and Air Balloons**
The Civil War occurred during the Industrial Revolution and included many innovations in technology. Many people call this the "first modern war" because of the movement from wooden ships and muskets to armored steamships and long range rifles.

On the Web

This is an eyewitness account of the Battle of Gettysburg from a teenage girl who lived in the town of Gettysburg. It is graphic, so pre-read: http://www.eyewitness-tohistory.com/gtburg.htm

Famous Folks

Walt Whitman, the famous American poet, was turning 42 when the Civil War broke out. He never enlisted but he did serve as a volunteer nurse at the front. His most famous poems are his volume *Leaves of Grass*, self-published in 1855. He also wrote the famous *Oh Captain! My Captain!* on the death of President Lincoln.

Additional Layer

In 1863 President Lincoln issued the Emancipation Proclamation as a war measure. It declared slaves in rebellious states free and allowed black men to join the Union army as well as making the outlawing of slavery a war goal.

This angered the Southerners who denounced it as uncivilized and who retaliated by declaring that any black men who were captured in battle would be tried as slave insurrectionists, the sentence of death being automatic.

It also resulted in tragedies like the Fort Pillow Massacre, where victorious Confederate soldiers brutally massacred the black regiments who were attempting to surrender.

Learn more.

Writer's Workshop

Expand the Clara Barton activity by having your child write a biography of Clara Barton's life.

For very young kids a few sentences is enough. By fifth grade they can write a page and by ninth grade a three page paper is not too much to expect. Have them read their report.

Ironclads, submarine technology, rifles, telegraph, railroads, photography, hot air balloons, naval mines, and torpedoes were developed during this time.

Choose one of these innovations and research more about it. Create a project relating to your research. Include how the technology was used during the Civil War as well as what modern technologies the innovation led to in today's world.

☺ ☺ **EXPLORATION: Map of Major Battles**

At the end of this unit you will find a printable map of Civil War Battles. Color one element of the map at a time as you explain the progress of the Civil War using the numbered items below.

Civil War Battles
April 1861 - April 1865

Each number below corresponds to a number on the map. So, as you read about the naval blockade the kids should color the naval blockade and then label it with the name and the dates. Color a campaign according to which side initiated it or a battle the color representing the side that won - blue for the North and red for the South.

1. **Border and Labels-** Color the border between north and south. Color the rivers and the ocean light blue. Label the Ohio, Mississippi, Missouri, Arkansas, and Red rivers.

2. **Naval Blockade 1861-65** Beginning in April of 1861 the Union forces used 500 ships to blockade 3,500 miles of southern coast from Texas to Virginia. During the war British blockade runners attempted to get past the blockade to trade supplies to the South for cotton.

3. **Mississippi Campaign 1861-63** Early in the war the Union moved to secure the Mississippi River by moving south from Tennessee and north from the Gulf of Mexico simultaneously. In a series of battles over a period of years they took control of the entire river with the exception of the city of Vicksburg.

4. **Peninsula Campaign Mar-Jul 1862** The Northern armies moved south toward Richmond, the new capital of the Confederacy, to try to take the city and end the rebellion quickly. In spite of superior numbers, equipment, and training, they were out-generalled by Robert E. Lee and the North was repulsed.

5. **Northern Virginia Campaign Aug-Sept 1862** Lee followed up his victory by marching on Washington. The Second Battle of Bull Run was won by the South and Washington barely saved.

6. **Antietam Sept 17, 1862** In the bloodiest single day in American military history 22,717 men were killed or wounded. This was the first battle on Union soil. The South was greatly outnumbered, so even though the North was poorly led, it was a victory for the Union.

7. **Emancipation Proclamation Sept 22, 1862** (effective Jan 1863) Lincoln had waited to give this Proclamation until the North had a victory. It was a military measure as well as humanitarian to officially link slavery to the war and the South. This link prevented France and Britain from aiding the South since neither country could be seen to support slavery, even though both countries would have liked to see a weak and divided United States.

8. **Battle of Fredericksburg Dec 11-15, 1862** The Union attacked entrenched Confederate positions repeatedly, taking more than twice as many casualties as the South, resulting in a Confederate win.

9. **Battle of Chancellorsville May 1863** Though the Confederates were more than twice outnumbered, Lee divided his men audaciously. Hooker, the Union general, was overly cautious and Lee took the day. But the victory was costly and the south could not replace the lost men. This was a devastating

Famous Folks

During the Civil War, Jonathan Letterman instituted the ambulance corps and field hospital methods still used today in the military.

Famous Folks

Mathew Brady brought his mobile photography studio and darkroom to the site of the great battles of the Civil War. He and his assistants created thousands of images, bringing the war home to northern households. He also took portraits of ordinary soldiers and important generals and politicians on both sides.

This photo at the Antietam Battlefield was taken by Alexander Gardner, who worked for Brady.

Famous Folks

Ulysses S. Grant was a general known for accepting horrific losses in order to win. He became the strength of the Northern war effort and later was elected president.

Famous Folks

Stand Watie was born in Cherokee land in Georgia to wealthy slave-owning plantation parents. He was forced with his family to move west with the Indian Removal Act in 1835. Hoping the Confederacy would support a free Cherokee nation, Watie sided with the South and became a Brigadier General. He led hundreds of successful battles and raids west of the Mississippi during the war.

loss to the North. Stonewall Jackson was killed by friendly fire during this battle.

10. **Siege of Vicksburg May 19-July 4, 1863** A Union victory, this gave complete Union control of the Mississippi, cutting off the western Confederacy.

11. **Gettysburg July 1-3 1863** Following recent wins, Lee decided to take the battle into northern territory. His gamble failed. It was a Union victory. All hope of foreign help was gone. Many count this, along with Vicksburg (both on the same day), as the turning point of the war.

12. **Chattanooga Oct-Nov 1863** The Union moved south toward Chattanooga, fighting battles as they went. They took Chattanooga, a vital rail hub and supply center for the South.

13. **Red River Campaign 1864** The Union moved up and down the Red River Valley to control the Red River region and eastern Texas. It was a failure and had little influence on the war.

14. **Overland Campaign May-Jun 1864** Grant takes command of Union troops. Sherman given command in the west. The Union headed south to take northern Virginia. This is when the Battle of the Wilderness and Battle of Spotsylvania Courthouse took place; both led to the siege of Petersburg.

15. **Sherman Atlanta Campaign Summer 1864** From Chattanooga, Sherman marched south to take Atlanta, another railway hub. Atlanta was besieged and fell in September. There were dozens of battles and skirmishes; the South fought back bitterly. The victory boosted Lincoln for re-election in 1864.

16. **Sherman's March To the Sea Nov 15-Dec 21, 1864** Sherman split his troops into several divisions to cover more ground and speed the march. The path of the armies was marked by destruction of factories, depots, railway lines, bridges, telegraph lines, and burning cities. Sherman operated deep in enemy territory and without supply lines, seizing food from the population as he went. He was met with resistance, but the campaign was militarily successful. It left the South devastated. Former slaves followed the army camp in the thousands, some of them joining the military effort.

17. **Siege of Petersburg June 1864-March 1864** A northern victory, this left the way open to Richmond, the capital.

18. **Carolina Campaign 1865** After a month rest at Savannah, Sherman marched his troops north through the Carolinas to link up with the federal troops in Virginia. Troops split into several groups to cover more ground and confuse the defense of the southern troops. Destruction, burning, and devastation followed the army, as did throngs of freed slaves and freed prisoners of war.

19. **Surrender at Appomattox Courthouse April 9, 1865-** Lee surrendered to General Grant. Within the next few weeks the remaining southern generals each surrendered.

☺ ☺ EXPLORATION: Reconstruction

After the South was defeated the federal government set terms the Southern states had to meet in order to be admitted back into the Union. They also reorganized and controlled the state governments of the rebellious states, sometimes with military governments, and enforced enfranchisement of the former slaves. This period of time from 1865 to 1877 is known as the Reconstruction Period.

It was during this time that the Ku Klux Klan was first organized and used to persecute and terrorize black and white Republicans. Eventually their tactics, and other more above board tactics, worked, and the rich white Southerners regained control of their governments by 1877, instituting Jim Crow laws.

Reconstruction was supposed to rebuild the South economically, give equality to the former slaves, and stabilize the Southern governments in line with the United States Constitution. But it didn't work. In 1877 the South was backward, poor, lacking basic services like schools and roads, and still a place of rampant racism and oppression. It would be another hundred years before blacks were no longer systematically denied basic rights in the South.

To find out why Reconstruction was such a challenge, read the links to documents from this page: https://www.civilwar.org/learn/educators/curriculum/high-school/african-americans-after-civil-war

What were the problems? What do you think the North could have done to turn former enemies into friends? Was it even possible?

Use the Reconstruction printable from the end of this unit. Cut out the title and glue it to another sheet of paper. Cut out the large rectangle on the solid lines and then cut into flaps on the solid lines. Fold along the dotted line. Glue the center strip to the sheet of paper with the title. Research each term on the flaps and write the definition under the flap. Draw a simple illustration on each flap as well.

Fabulous Fact

The Red Badge of Courage is set at Chancellorsville, as is the movie *Gods and Generals* (PG-13).

Library List

The 1993 movie, Gettysburg (PG), is six hours long, but worth the time to watch if you have kids in the middle grades and older.

Fabulous Fact

In the west the Confederacy did not have resources to properly execute the war. Independent guerrilla bands like Quantrill's Raiders took to attacking farms, government officials, small towns, and unarmed soldiers on leave, terrorizing the country.

In August of 1863 the raiders attacked the town of Lawrence, Kansas, killing 164 civilian men and boys and burning most of the town. This, of course, led to further violence.

Learn more about Quantrill's Raiders.

GEOGRAPHY: NATIONAL PARKS

Fabulous Facts

The national parks contain both the highest (Denali) and the lowest (Death Valley) points in North America.

Additional Layer

Most of the national parks are beautiful because of the underlying rock formations formed by magma, volcanoes, glaciers, wind, and water. Research further into the geology of one of your favorite parks.

This rock formation in Arches National Park was created by wind power.

On the Web

If you do plan a visit to a national park or historic site, grab one of their lesson plans ahead of time: https://www.nps.gov/teachers/index.htm

The first national park in the world was created in 1872 at Yellowstone. A national park exists to preserve the natural scenery and wildlife in tact for posterity. National parks are also a source of national pride and a place for visitors to come and see the natural beauties of the country.

Wyoming, Montana, and Idaho were still territories when Yellowstone was created. As territories, not states, they were controlled by the federal government. The federal government took control of the land, hence Yellowstone was a "national" park. Since then dozens of parks have been set aside in the United States, both for the preservation of the natural world and for the preservation of historical sites. They are all run by the National Park Service and administered under the Department of the Interior.

😊 😊 😊 **EXPLORATION: Map of the National Parks**
At the end of this unit you will find a printable map of the national parks. Color in the national parks. Color in the stars, which represent national historical parks.

National Parks of the United States

😊 😊 😊 **EXPEDITION: Visit a National Park**
Plan a trip to a national park or national historic site near you. Learn something of the history and the natural wonders of the park before you go.

😊 😊 **EXPLORATION: Theodore Roosevelt & John Muir**
In May of 1903, when Theodore Roosevelt was president of the United States, he traveled to Yosemite Valley in California. He went on a three day camping trip with John Muir, a writer who had influentially been cam-

paigning for the idea that wild places ought to be set aside and preserved for future generations. During the camping trip the two men, both avid outdoorsmen in their different ways, talked about their visions for the future regarding the wild spaces of the nation. John Muir pled again that some places be preserved and kept pristine.

He made his case well because in the next few years Roosevelt would sign into law the 1906 Act for Preservation of American Antiquities and the 1906 Yosemite Recession Bill. The Antiquities Act made it possible for the president to unilaterally declare land and historical sites restricted for use, such as when creating a national monument from federal land. The process to create a national park goes through Congress and therefore takes longer. The Yosemite Recession Bill gave the land that is now the Yosemite Valley to the federal government from the State of California so that the federal government could administer the area as a national park.

Make a "campfire" and set it in the center of your living room (You can also just set several candles in the center of your group and have them be your campfire). Sit everyone around it and tell stories about Teddy Roosevelt, John Muir, or the national parks. See the Library List for book ideas, look up stories on the Internet, or tell what you already know.

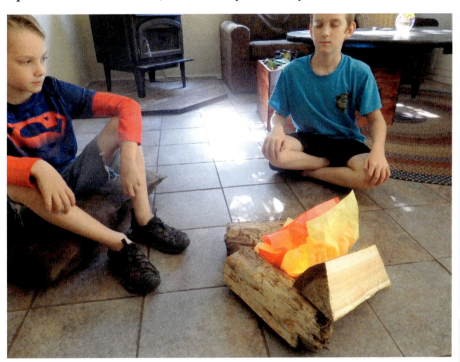

To make a campfire, start with several logs. Stack them log cabin style. Coil white Christmas lights or battery powered tea candles down inside the logs. Stuff red and yellow tissue paper into the center with corners sticking up like flames. Turn the lights on. It feels magical indoors with the lights off, especially if you also set up a tent. You can pitch a small tent indoors if you like or just make a tent out of a sheet.

Famous Folks

John Muir was a Scottish-American naturalist and the father of the National Park System.

He petitioned Congress to preserve some of the wild lands of the west, including Yosemite, to protect them from exploitation.

Writer's Workshop

Make two lists. One should include the national parks you most want to visit. The other should include national parks you have already visited. You can call them "bucket list" and "been there, done that."

On the Web

This YouTube channel has dozens of videos about the national parks of America.

https://www.youtube.com/user/58NationalParks

Additional Layer

Yellowstone is an active supervolcano, one of only a handful on earth. A supervolcano is capable of sending out ejecta greater than 240 cubic miles in volume, thousands of times larger than a normal volcano like Mt. Pinatubo or Mount St. Helens. Mount St. Helens ejecta was a mere .7 cubic miles.

Hot steam pouring from caves and holes in the ground in Yellowstone are evidence of its volcanic tendencies.

Fabulous Fact

Park rangers have many different roles. They give interpretive talks to visitors, monitor wildlife, fight fires, study cultural artifacts, manage campgrounds, man fee booths, control traffic, act as law enforcement, and rescue hurt or lost visitors.

☺ ☺ ☺ EXPLORATION: National Park Touring Company

Choose one of the national parks or national historic parks, and learn more about it online or in books. Then make a travel guide booklet as though you are a touring company taking people through the park. Include a map of how to get to the park, a map of the park itself, and pages about the major features or attractions of the park. You may also want to include information about where to stay or where to eat.

☺ ☺ EXPLORATION: Video Tour of the National Parks

Choose a national park or national historic park and create a video tour of the park. You can use slideshow or video editing software. Include photographs of the park, a map of the park, and a little about the history of the park. Create a script and narrate your video.

☺ ☺ ☺ EXPLORATION: Most Popular Park Award

Find out how many visitors pass through each of the national parks (exclude the national historic sites) and make a graph showing the numbers. Which park is the most popular in the U.S.A.?

This is the Copher family at Crater Lake National Park in Oregon. This is a beautiful park, but not nearly so crowded as Yellowstone or Yosemite.

☺ ☺ ☺ EXPLORATION: National Park Art Gallery

The national parks contain some of the most stunning scenery on earth, and so they have been the subject of many artists' paintings and photographs. You can create a national park art gallery on a wall in your house. Find art of the national parks from one of the artists below, print out a few examples, mount them on larger paper, create captions for the art saying who painted or photographed them and what the scene is, then place them on your walls to make a gallery or in a binder to create a national parks art book.

Artists to choose among:

Painters
Albert Bierstadt
Thomas Moran
Chiura Obata
George Catlin
William Henry Jackson
Mark Gudmundsen

Photographers
Ansel Adams
Iwao Matshushita

This photograph by Ansel Adams (1942) depicts Grand Teton National Park in Wyoming. Art like this helped convince Americans to preserve wild lands.

😊 😊 😊 EXPLORATION: Preserving the Parks

The national parks spend a lot of time and effort teaching their visitors to preserve the parks. There are cultural artifacts (Native American and pioneer) and natural treasures (water, trees, air, wildlife, and land) to preserve for future generations.

When you visit national parks or other wild lands there are some things you can do to make sure the parks stay as beautiful or even better than they are now.

1. Always take care of your trash responsibly. Put it in trash cans or recycling bins, and never carelessly leave it on the ground. If you come

Fabulous Fact

Artists still set up their easels and tripods in national parks. This woman is painting a scene in Yellowstone.

Additional Layer

Conservation is focused on maintaining the health of the natural world by using natural resources responsibly and in such a way that they are in tact for future generations.

Preservation, by contrast, is the protection of natural landscapes, buildings, or sites from use of any kind.

There was a big conflict between conservationists and preservationists in the early 20th century. Read up about John Muir (a preservationist) and Gifford Pinchot (a conservationist) to learn about the beliefs and aims of each side.

Which side do you think won? Is there still a conflict between these two viewpoints? Which viewpoint do you mostly agree with? Do you think there is a place for both?

Additional Layer

The National Park Service administers national historic sites as well as parks. This is the National Maritime Museum in San Francisco.

Most of the national parks are in the west, but most of the national historic sites are in the east.

Find a historic site near you and learn more about it. Why has it been preserved?

Additional Layer

The national parks don't just preserve the land, they also preserve and protect the animals like the bison, once close to extinction, but now thriving in places like Yellowstone National Park.

What other animals can you see in national parks? Have you spotted any?

across someone else's trash, pick it up.

2. Don't feed or try to touch animals. Animals that become dependent on people food are far less healthy and far less safe than if they remain wild.
3. Don't deface buildings, trees, rocks, or anything else.
4. Stay on roads or trails that are created for people. Your feet may not really do much damage to a meadow, but thousands of people trampling over it will ruin its beauty for decades.
5. Obey warning signs. Hundreds of people have been killed or injured because they climbed boulders or walked past the barriers.

Think about each of these rules and why they are rules. Decide for yourself that you will always be responsible in nature. Make an illustrated poster of these rules.

Yellowstone National Park is one of the places you want to stay on the path. That beautiful blue water is deadly.

🙂 🙂 🙂 **EXPLORATION: National Parks Mission Statement**

"The National Park Service preserves unimpaired the natural and cultural resources and values of the National Park System for the enjoyment, education, and inspiration of this and future generations. The Park Service cooperates with partners to extend the benefits of natural and cultural resource conservation and outdoor recreation throughout this country and the world." -National Park Mission Statement

The mission of the NPS is always a positive one, celebrating the good things about America and the challenges Americans have overcome. The national parks help Americans to define who they are as a people.

When you go to any national park today you can hear languages from all over the world spoken. A few years ago we camped in Yellowstone next to Belgians. On a recent trip to Yosemite we heard German and Japanese spoken. When we visited the Maritime Museum in San Francisco we were in a tour group with a British family. While America's national parks are definitely uniquely American, they are also for all people. They are for all Americans and for the rest of the world too.

It is interesting that in this one place we find it possible to use and exploit nature and also preserve and protect it for our posterity. In fact, the use of the parks, the interest and funds they generate, are what makes preservation possible.

Learn what people are doing today to preserve and protect the national parks. On a poster board or a sheet of card stock draw the National Park Service arrowhead emblem. Visit the NPS website to see it. Around the arrowhead write short paragraphs describing the different people who work to fulfill the mission of the parks. You can include park rangers, volunteers, the National Parks Conservation Association, and the National Park Foundation.

You can be a volunteer in the National Parks: https://www.nps.gov/getinvolved/volunteer.htm.

☺ ☺ ☺ EXPLORATION: National Landmarks

One of the reasons national parks are important is to preserve the most beautiful places in nature. At the end of this unit you will find a printable featuring five landmarks that are protected by national parks. To complete the printable you will have to do some research about each of these landmarks. First cut out the title and glue it to the top of another piece of paper. Then cut out the large rectangle piece and along the center dividing lines up to the dotted line to create flaps. Glue the edge of the large rectangle (the side behind the dashed line) to the paper with your title. On the flap draw a picture of each landmark. Under flap write facts about each landmark. Include which national park it can be found in and other interesting things you learn about it.

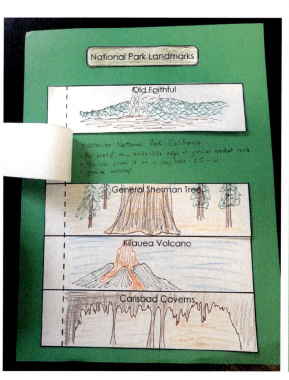

On the Web

Most national parks have a Junior Ranger program where kids can earn badges for completing the activities in a booklet.

The program is intended to create a new generation of Americans who understand and care about our natural resources. There are some activities you can do online from home: https://www.nps.gov/kids/jr-Rangers.cfm

On the Web

Watch this 45 minute video from PBS about the history of the National Parks, *This is America*: http://www.pbs.org/nationalparks/about/this-is-america/

Famous Folks

General Phillip Sheridan, of Civil War and Plains Wars fame, fought for the protection of Yellowstone, which was being irresponsibly hunted by adventurers and exploited by developers and the railroads.

When Congress stripped the funding for the park Sheridan took his troops in and administered and policed the park until the National Park Service was formed in 1916.

SCIENCE: PLATE TECTONICS

Teaching Tip

In Unit 1-6 we learned a little bit about plate tectonics in Geography. We're going to review and build on what we learned about the earth in this unit.

On The Web

Mr. Anderson teaches plate tectonic theory to middle school and high school kids. http://youtu.be/JmC-vjQGSNM

On The Web

This interactive game and learning tool teaches about plate tectonic theory, sliding plates, and the structure of the earth, which we'll get into more in the next unit. http://www.learner.org/interactives/dynamicearth/drift.html

Writer's Workshop

Research the evidence that geologists have found that there was a super continent at one time. You may also want to research a dissenting opinion. Take notes and arrange the notes in a logical order. Make an argument for or against the idea based on your research. Write it up in a research paper. Be sure to create a bibliography of your sources.

In the 1960s scientists established a theory about the continents on earth. They decided the great plates that make up the continents were not fixed, but rather were drifting. They were drifting so much that at one time there had been only one super continent. They named this super continent Pangaea. In the interim, the geography of the world has drastically changed over long periods of time until now we have seven distinct continents; actually six, Europe and Asia are considered separate continents, but are really one land mass.

Of course this is all theory, there's no real way, at present at least, to absolutely prove any such thing really happened. But scientists have observed that the Atlantic Ocean gets a little bigger each year and the Pacific a little smaller, by a few millimeters. They also noticed how the coastlines of Africa and South America look like they ought to fit together.

There have been other clues supporting continental drift as well, including India pushing into Asia hard enough to form the Himalayas Mountains, the Great Rift Valley in Africa threatening to become the next continental split, and the great deep valleys and high mountain ranges of the oceans. Scientists have more evidence too. Magnetic field reversals that change the polarity of the earth are common. Furthermore, similar fossils have been found on continents now separated by oceans. But the real kicker in driving this whole the earth's-crust-is-floating-and-moving-around theory was the understanding of how plates could move under each other.

☺ ☺ ☺ EXPLORATION: Pangaea

Pangaea is a geological concept of what the landmasses on earth might have looked like long ago. The continents, or more precisely the plates, are moving. We can tell that pretty definitely at this point. The forces involved are fairly massive and a little on the complex side, so no one knows what the continents might have looked like exactly when they were all shoved together in the past. To the right you can see one idea though.

Image by Kieff, CC licence, Wikimedia

To make a Pangaea craft you'll need three paper plates or three pieces of card stock, a map of the earth as it is today, some acrylic or tempera paints, and some paintbrushes.

1. On the first plate paint a freehand map of the earth with green continents and blue oceans.
2. On the second plate paint a freehand version of the continents sort of squished together, but still recognizable as continents we know today.
3. On the third plate paint a "super continent" that you envision as Pangaea. Make the continents fit together into one landmass.
4. Once the paint dries, label each plate: "Earth Today," "Separating Continents," and "Pangaea."
5. Fold each plate in half from the north pole to the south. Then glue the plates together to make a mobile.
6. Hang it by a string from your ceiling.

☺ ☻ EXPLORATION: Cracking Continents

The crust of the earth is cold and hard, a brittle crust over a plastic molten planet. Brittle things break.

Make some sugar cookie dough and let the kids each shape their own super continent. Bake the cookies until they are dark and crispy. Once they've cooled for ten minutes break the cookies into "continents." It's fine if the continents look nothing like the real continents of today. Then decorate the continents with green frosting.

You can go further and let the kids make their own world on a paper plate with blue frosting water, chocolate chip mountains, dark green dyed coconut for jungles, yellow decorating sugar for deserts, and so on.

Talk about how the crust is hard and breaks apart like the cookies. Explain that underneath the crust is molten rock and plastic (not completely solid,

Additional Layer

Scientific disciplines have "unifying theories," or overall ideas that explain how everything else within that discipline works. The unifying theory of geology is plate tectonics.

Plate tectonics explains the cause of earthquakes and volcanoes, the formation of new rock, the islands and valleys and mountain ranges on the surface of the earth, how rocks are formed and why there is such great variety of rocks, and the rock cycle.

If plate tectonics is proven wrong, it will destroy all the other knowledge about geologic processes that we have. Unifying theories are then, very important to their discipline.

What are some unifying theories in other fields? Do a little research.

On the Web

Watch the YouTube video "Plate Tectonics: Evidence of Pate Movement" from Khan Academy.

You can treat videos like this as though they are a lecture and require your kids to take notes. Then create a quiz as well.

Fabulous Fact

In the early 1900s there was a vehement debate between "drifters" who thought the plates of earth were moving and "fixists" who thought the continents were static. The person to start the debate was Alfred Wegener who cited the similar rock structure of the Newfoundland and Scotland highlands and the Caledonian and Appalachian Ranges as evidence that they had once been joined. But Wegener could not provide a mechanism by which continental rock could plow through oceanic rock, and so he wasn't taken seriously by most scientists. Intriguingly, there is still not a definite mechanism known by which this happens, but the evidence that it does happen has mounted until the theory of plate tectonics is generally accepted by scientists.

On the Web

This site has a cool interactive map where you can explore the plates of the earth, learn more about plate tectonics, and then take a quiz to test your knowledge. https://www.geolsoc.org.uk/Plate-Tectonics/

but not really liquid). The molten material allows for movement of these plates, which are less dense than oceanic crust and therefore "float" over the top of the ocean plates.

☺ ☺ ☺ EXPLORATION: How Do Plates Move?

We learned in Unit 4-6 that the crust of the earth is really very thin, like the peel on an apple, but still, the earth is a very large massive rock and even a thin little peel of a crust is going to be heavy. Why do the plates move at all? Why don't they just sit there floating on the molten material beneath?

Some people think the answer is that the molten stuff isn't sitting still either. The movement of the hot rock under the crust and massive convection currents arising clear from the core creates shifting underneath. That translates to lots of shifting on the surface. It all happens because of some simple laws of physics that recognize that heat rises and cold sinks.

Below is a diagram of a convection cell in the mantle of the earth. The arrows show how material is flowing. The flowing material pulls things around it along, such as the surface plates. You also have pushing from the places where new crust material is being formed.

Other people say the convection currents in the earth are nowhere nearly strong enough to move plates, especially when the plates meet great obstacles. For example, think of the

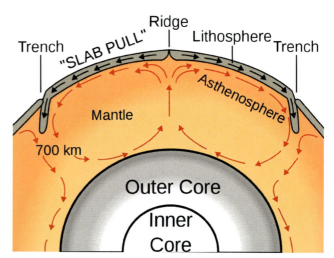

forces that would be needed to form the Himalayas. These scientists are floating (ha ha) a theory that the plates themselves are responsible for their own movement. They say one end of the plate is pulled under by its own weight, creating a rift on its other end where new material can rise up and harden into new rock. As plates get older they also get denser and more compressed, meaning they are ready to sink. So the edges of the ocean near the continents are the oldest rock. It sinks and slides under the continent.

Of course, it could be a combination of the two theories or something else completely. Do you think convection explains mountain ranges like the Andes and Himalayas? Do you think plate pull can explain the forces needed for these mountain building activities?

Science isn't all about doing experiments; it's also about thinking and coming up with questions. Draw a labeled diagram of each theory behind why the plates move. Then write questions about each theory that you have. Discuss your ideas with a group.

☺ ☺ ☺ EXPLORATION: Zones on the Edge

At the edges of plates is where most of the interesting action happens. Use the "Plate Boundaries" worksheet from the end of this unit to color and highlight three main types of plate zones: convergent, divergent, and transform faults.

Convergent Plates are plates that are coming together, moving toward each other. This could include two oceanic plates, such as in the Mid-Pacific Trench. It could also be two continental plates, such as where India and Asia have collided to form the Himalayas. And finally, convergent plates can include an oceanic and a continental plate, as on the west coast of the United States. In this case, the lighter and thicker continental plate will ride over the top of the oceanic plate, which is thinner and more dense.

Often along the boundaries of these plates there will be volcanic activity. This is how the Cascade Range in the Pacific Northwest was formed, including active volcanoes like Mount Rainier and Mount St. Helens.

Divergent Plate zones are spreading or moving away from each other. This can happen in a fault between two oceanic plates or in the middle of a continental plate. The Mid-Atlantic Ridge is formed by a divergent zone as is the Great Rift Valley in Africa.

Transform faults are places where the plates are sliding horizontally past each other instead of one sliding under the other. These happen in oceanic crust on the sea floor and in continental crust. The San Andreas Fault in California is the most well-known example. Earthquakes often take place in these zones. Almost on a daily basis tremors can be felt as the tension between the plates builds and slips. Some of these are just small tremors, but some are much larger.

Famous Folks

Ted Irving of Canada was the first scientist to provide hard evidence for the theory of continental drift. He studied paleomagnetism, the history of the earth's magnetic field and the way it had flipped over long eons of time. The successive bands of flipped magnetic sections on the ocean floor gave evidence that the sea floor was spreading.

Fabulous Fact

As new oceanic plate material is formed it has quite a bit of iron in it. Iron, as you know, responds to magnetic forces. It is easily magnetized. The earth is one big magnet (see Unit 4-6 to learn more). So when new material spews out of the ocean vents and cools into new rock the iron in the rock aligns with the magnetic poles of the earth. Pretty cool.

Here is a video that explains how magnetism is related to sea flood spreading: https://www.youtube.com/watch?v=BCzCmldiaWQ

On the Web

Watch this video about the types of faults: https://www.youtube.com/watch?v=rjn2ZJw-pqQA

Fabulous Fact

Some parts of the sea floor are more magnetic than others. Rock that cools more quickly has smaller crystals and is more easily magnetized. Rock that cools more slowly will have less and less magnetism.

Famous Folks

Maurice Ewing was an American oceanographer who mapped the sea floor, discovering the mid-ocean ridges, during World War II. His work was instrumental to the theory of plate tectonics.

On the Web

Maurice Ewing performed most of his research from aboard a nav research vessel called the Atlantis. Since the 1940s there have been a series of vessels with the same name all performing oceanic research. You can read about the current vessel here: http://oceanexplorer.noaa.gov/technology/vessels/atlantis/atlantis.html

☺ ☺ ☺ EXPLORATION: Mid-Atlantic Ridge

The Mid-Atlantic Ridge is a place where a rift in the plates formed long ago. New seafloor forms in this area and from there the seafloor spreads both east and west, making the Atlantic Ocean a few centimeters larger each year.

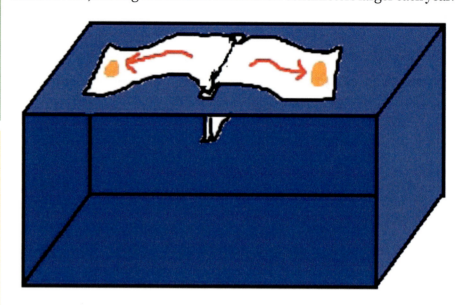

Make a model showing how this works. You need a shoe box, two pieces of paper, scissors, and some lumps of clay.

1. Cut a slit in the center bottom of the shoe box, about two centimeters wide and long enough for your paper to slip through easily.
2. Put your two pieces of paper through the slit and hold down the upper edges, one on the left and one on the right, with the lumps of clay.
3. Slowly slide the paper up through the slit in the box.

The slit represents a "fault" or crack in a plate where material from inside the earth can well up. The paper represents plates that are growing as new material is formed. Notice that though the outer edges of the plates are weighted down and mostly flat, the area near the "fault" bulges up. This happens in real life too; remember it's called the Mid-Atlantic Ridge, not the Mid-Alantic Canyon. Forces from other big plates keep the plate from moving away from the ridge, making the oceanic plates move more slowly away from the center than the new acquisition of material would normally dictate. They can't flow away smoothly, so they build up quite a bit. This results in huge underwater mountain ranges. Iceland is the top of one of these underwater mountain ranges formed by the Mid-Atlantic Ridge, and as you would guess, Iceland is very volcanic.

☺ EXPLORATION: Pacific Trenches

In the Pacific Ocean and in a few other places under the sea there are deep trenches along the edges of plates that are being subducted under other plates, either other oceanic or under continental plates.

Subduction of plates occurs at an angle. The plate being pulled underneath descends at an angle, not straight down and not horizontally. And volcanoes form at about 200 miles from the surface trench, on the side where the plate is being subducted.

This is exactly what is happening along the coast of South America. The Nazca Plate, an oceanic plate, is being subducted underneath the South American Plate, a continental plate. All along the coast of South America a deep trench has formed. The plate then descends at an angle underneath the continent of South America and a large mountain range of volcanoes has formed all along the coast of that continent, the Andes Mountains, about 200 miles inland from the trench.

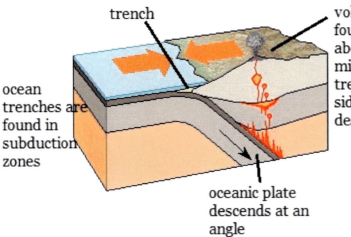

trench

volcanoes are found in a zone about 200 miles from the trench on the side the trench descends into.

ocean trenches are found in subduction zones

oceanic plate descends at an angle

How do we know the trench descends at an angle like that? We can look at the data from the epicenters of volcanic activity along this very active coast line and see some interesting things happening. Make a 3-D map of the South American coastline to plot the epicenters of these quakes, and you too will see the plate descending.

At the end of this unit you will find a map of the South American coastline and a table of data showing the epicenters of some major quakes. The table shows where the quakes occurred in terms of longitude and latitude and also how deep they were under the surface of the earth.

Print the map out and glue it onto one side of a cardboard box, medium sized, bigger than a shoe box, smaller than a packing crate. (If you have really big feet a shoe box will probably work). Poke a pin through at each of the places where a quake occurs, so you can see the spot from the underside of the map. Then dangle a string through the hole, longer strings for deeper quakes. Mold a ball of clay around each of the strings to weigh it down. When you are finished plotting each of the quakes on your 3-D map you will have a good view of how the plate is descending.

Additional Layer

You probably don't think of Oregon and Washington as earthquake zones, but the two states are sitting right along the Cascadia fault line. This is a deep fault line in a subduction zone just off the coast. When it goes the results will be a massive tsunami. Watch this documentary: https://www.youtube.com/watch?v=VR95-T6D-vQM

Famous Folks

Hugo Benioff and Kiyoo Wadati were seismologists who charted deep earthquakes along plate margins in the Pacific Ocean, noticing that the epicenters follow a slanted trajectory, getting deeper as you move further inland. These slanted subduction zones are called Wadati-Benioff zones.

Kiyoo Wadati of Japan.

Famous Folks

Robert Dietz and Harry Hess, both American geophysicists and oceanographers, conducted research into seafloor spreading, coining the term in the early 1960s. Their findings revolutionized the way people saw the geologic processes of earth.

Famous Folks

The geophysicist who finally put the whole theory of plate tectonics together was Canadian John Tuzo Wilson.

Photo by Stephen Morris, CC license, Wikimedia

He first described and named transform faults like the San Andreas and hot spots like the one under Hawaii.

The whole concept of seabed expansion and contraction (the moving sea floor) is called the Wilson Cycle after him.

☺ ☻ EXPLORATION: Map the Plates

Using a map of the world from the end of this unit and a student atlas that shows the plate margins around the world, draw lines on your map at the plate margins. Label each of the plates. Draw arrows along your plate margins that show which direction the plates are moving.

Cut apart your plates with scissors. Move them around to show how the continents and oceans might look a million years from now. Where do you think continents might split apart? Where will the next mountain ranges form? Where do you think new volcanic islands might emerge? Will any lands move into a new climate zone?

☺ ☻ EXPLORATION: Plate Movement

Prepare a batch of red gelatin and pour it into a large rectangular pan (a casserole dish or cookie sheet). Let the gelatin solidify in the fridge for a few hours. Then have the kids wash their hands really well. Use graham crackers to simulate the crustal plates. Demonstrate each of the major ways plates move past each other using the graham crackers.

- Convergent (plates smashing into each other)
- Divergent (plates spreading apart from each other)
- Transverse (plates sliding past each other)
- Subductive (one plate sliding under another plate)

As you manipulate your graham cracker plates, notice how the gelatin "magma" behaves. What do you think is happening when the gelatin wells up between the plates? See if the kids can identify which type of movement is happening as you (or another child) demonstrate different types of plate movements.

☺ ☻ EXPLORATION: Ring of Fire

Watch this video about the Ring of Fire: https://www.youtube.com/watch?v=uw7Uq137YJQ

While you watch, take notes. Use the "Ring of Fire Notes" printable from the end of this unit. There are three major headings under which to take notes. Write down what you learn from the video in each of these sections. Include quick labeled sketches where appropriate.

After the video, on the left of the vertical line write a few key words or questions next to your notes that help you remember key points. Then write a summary of the information from the video in one or two sentences at the bottom of the page.

Study your notes by covering the detailed information on the right with your hand or with another piece of paper, using the key words on the left side to jog your memory. Practice repeating back the information you wrote until you can remember it easily.

Finally take the Ring of Fire Quiz from the printables at the end of this unit, and see how you did. Watch the video again to check your answers. Could your notes have been better?

☺ ☻ EXPLORATION: New Plate Formation

As of right now the crust of the earth is broken up into fourteen plates. But new plates are forming; new cracks in the crust are appearing even now. One of the most profound places this is happening is in East Africa along the Rift Valley.

Read this article about the East African Rift: http://geology.com/articles/east-africa-rift.shtml

Make a model of the rift using salt dough or clay. Dry it according to directions on the package (if using clay) or let it air dry. Paint it and label it using toothpicks and paper flags. Explain the East African Rift and how it is forming to younger students.

Memorization Station

Look up and memorize the definitions of these terms:

Plate

Divergent boundary

Convergent boundary

Transform boundary

Subduction zone

Rift valley

Mid-ocean ridge

Seafloor spreading

Pangaea

Teaching Tip

The Ring of Fire note taking and quiz are practice for how to take notes from a video or lecture, a skill kids will need in college and often on the job.

The printable we provided practices the Cornell method of taking notes, which you can learn more about here: https://www.youtube.com/watch?v=WtW9I-yEo4OQ

You may want to have your student watch the video on note taking as well.

On the Web

Watch this clip about the East African Rift: https://www.youtube.com/watch?v=0cZYuBiVVYE

Arts: Post-Impressionism

Fabulous Fact

When you look at Post-Impressionist paintings side by side, you might feel that they have nothing in common. But there was one really important thing they had in common - they were all about optics, and especially about the way our eyes perceive light and color.

Their color mixing, interesting brush strokes, and dots of paint were all really just ways to play with our eyes. They combined light and color in new ways to make people look twice.

Additional Layer

The use of line changed pretty drastically between Impressionist and Post-Impressionist paintings. In most Impressionist paintings actual lines of paint were almost non-existent and could be described as "fuzzy" at best. But Post-Impressionists began to incorporate stronger lines again. Look at the outlined vase around Van Gogh's Sunflowers paintings. Thick lines like that never appeared in Impressionist paintings.

The art of the Post-Impressionist era didn't fit into a simple mold. It was not as much a true art movement as it was an era. It lasted from about 1885-1910. The artists of this time didn't all group together and create a recognizable style. They didn't have a list of common characteristics within their art. The post-Impressionist artists all veered off in their own ways and experimented with all kinds of styles and techniques. I suppose the thing they had in common is their individualism. They all experimented with all kinds of styles, throwing out anything that was left of traditional painting in Paris.

Although none of their paintings really have a strong resemblance to each other, you might notice a few things in common. You'll see a lot of color. Paintings from this time were not just shades of browns and grays and muted tones. They were bright. They used lots of different colors regardless of whether they looked realistic or not. Post-Impressionist painters also focused on geometric shapes a lot. The Impressionists before them had made their lines so blurry that you almost couldn't identify lines and shapes in many of their paintings at all, but Post-Impressionists returned to more solid looking lines and shapes. Some also began to experiment with creating the shapes and lines in different ways - like by making dots or swirls.

The name for the era, Post-Impressionism, came from an art critic named Roger Fry. He organized an art exhibition for many of these artists to come and show their work; it was called *Manet and the Post-Impressionists*. Manet himself was not a Post Impressionist; Fry was referring to all of the art since Manet as being Post-Impressionist.

The four most important Post-Impressionist painters were Paul Cézanne, Paul Gauguin, Vincent van Gogh, and Georges Seurat.

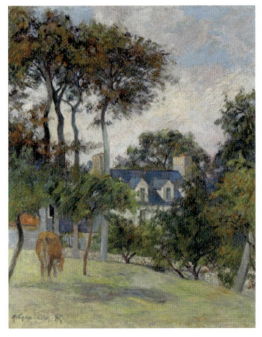

This landscape painting is called La Maison Blanche by Paul Gauguin.

☺ ☻ ☻ EXPLORATION: Playing With Shapes and Color

A lot of the the ideas of the Impressionist painters that came before them were rejected by the Post-Impressionists. Painters in France were looking for something new to evolve the work the Impressionists had begun when they rejected painting solely for the critics who judged them within famous salons. Post-Impressionists continued to be really interested in bright, strong colors. But, in general, they wanted their paintings to have more structure and feel more solid than the Impressionist paintings had.

This painting, The Centenary of Independence, by Henri Rousseau is a perfect example of the vivid colors and focus on shapes that many of the Post-Impressionists focused on. The paintings from this era look much more solid than the paintings of Impressionism. Can you pick out geometric shapes in the painting?

They began to see shapes within nature and focus on them. They saw geometry in the world and in nature.

Have you ever looked at a simple how to draw book for kids? Essentially, each item is broken down into its basic shapes.

Fabulous Fact

Often Post-Impressionism is called Neo-Impressionism. Post is another way to say "after" while neo is another way to say "new."

Post-Impressionists were the painters who came after the Impressionists and changed their style to make it new.

Additional Layer

Symbolism, primitivism, synthetism, pointillism, and neo-impressionism were are styles that fell under the umbrella of Post-Impressionist.

Find out the meanings of each of these words.

Famous Folks

Pablo Picasso and Henri Matisse called Paul Cézanne "the father of us all." He influenced modern painting profoundly.

Paul Cézanne's self portrait

Teaching Tip

Oil pastels can be tricky to work with, but they can produce vibrant works of art if you use them correctly. Here are a few tricks for oils pastels:

- Apply them heavily in one direction, then use a napkin to blend.

- Try out color mixing by applying a primary colored oil pastel first, then layering another color on top, and blending.

- Create a scratch art effect by layering two thickly applied colors, then using a paper clip to scrape away parts of the top color.

- A cotton swab dipped in baby oil acts like a paint thinner and allows you to spread and blend the colors.

In your sketchbook, draw two to three items that are made up of basic shapes. Accentuate the geometric shapes in your drawings. Several easy ones could be a sailboat, flower, buildings, or a mouse. Some more complex ones to try: a giraffe, a tree, a dog, or bicycle. Now add vibrant colors to your drawings. Although they weren't realistic looking, the Post-Impressionists loved to use colors that stood out.

☺ ☺ ☺ EXPLORATION: Cézanne's Tulips

Paul Cézanne is thought of as the leader of the Post-Impressionists. He was analytically minded, almost approaching art as a scientist would. He didn't just paint; he constructed. He loved to make still life paintings because he could examine the items from many angles, study them for a long time, and then paint them architecturally.

In Unit 4-6 about Impressionism we made a still life painting of apples in the style of Cézanne. As he progressed as an artist, he came away from the Impressionist style and bridged the gap between it and the more modern art of the Post-Impressionists.

He continued to paint many, many still life paintings. To make a tulip still life you'll need thick watercolor paper, oil pastels, baby oil, and a cotton swab.

Draw a picture of tulips in a vase using oil pastels. Think about the basic shapes of the vase and the flowers, and use those shapes as you draw. Scribble in the outlines with oil pastels. You don't need to worry about covering every spot with color. Now dip a a cotton swab in baby oil. Rub the cotton swab over the colorful parts, smearing and spreading the oil pastel within the outlines. Use a different cotton swab for each color or area. The oil will spread, blend, and brighten the colorful oil pastels.

☺ ☻ ☺ EXPLORATION: Van Gogh's Starry Night

Vincent Van Gogh's *Starry Night* is one of the most recognizable paintings to most kids.

Practice drawing the shapes Van Gogh used in your sketchbook. Divide your page into 4 boxes. Label each box - side to side, circles in circles, swirling lines, and curves. Within each box, practice those motions using oil pastels or crayons.

Once you've gotten the strokes down, you may want to make your own oil pastel *Starry Night* art in your sketchbook.

On The Web

Before making your *Starry Night* art, watch this beautiful representation of the movement of the painting set to music.

https://vimeo.com/36466564

Fabulous Facts

Post-Impressionism began in the 1880s. During the time the Post-Impressionists were painting. . .

- Susan B. Anthony and 50 other women were under arrest for voting
- Alexander Graham Bell invented the telephone
- Gottlieb Daimler built the first motorcycle by mounting a gas engine on a bicycle
- Public education was emerging
- Charles Darwin published *The Descent of Man*.

Fabulous Fact

Cézanne may be the father of Post-Impressionism and the most accomplished painter of his day, but Vincent van Gogh created the most recognizable paintings to us now.

☺ ☺ ☺ EXPLORATION: Sunflowers

Van Gogh's *Sunflower* painting is also very famous. Van Gogh was a pioneer in impasto painting. Impasto is a painting technique where paint is applied thickly and the brush strokes are visible. There is generally so much paint that it creates a texture on the painting; the surface is raised and bumpy from the paint. In the Van Gogh Museum in Amsterdam you can see a reproduction of Sunflowers that you are allowed to go up and touch. You can feel the bumpiness of the painted flowers.

Use a tiny 2" x 2" canvas to make your own sunflower impasto in miniature. Van Gogh's favorite color was yellow. Use at least four shades of yellow, along with greens and browns to create your sunflower. Thicken your acrylic paint by adding a little cornstarch to it so it will create a more textured look. Use thick, heavy brush strokes and lots of paint layers to create an impasto painting like Vincent Van Gogh did.

☺ ☺ EXPLORATION: Paul Gauguin

Paul Gauguin's life story sometimes overshadows his art. Dissatisfied with Europe and its art, Gauguin decided to leave his family to live a wild, single life in a tropical place. During those years he still wasn't really happy and tried unsuccessfully to commit suicide. He went to work on the Panama Canal for awhile, and then eventually went on to Tahiti and Marquesas. He painted lots of island scenes in really bright colors and simplistic shapes, completely throwing out all of the conventions of European paintings.

The style of those paintings ended up in much of his other work. We'll look at two of his paintings side by side and discuss them. These two are both self portraits, but they are very different from one another. He painted and sculpted over 40 self portraits, but we'll just look at two.

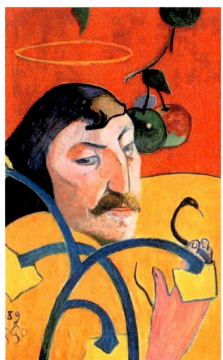

Discussion Questions:

- Describe the two styles. The one on the left looks more re-alistic while the second, on the right, looks like a caricature, which his friends called an "unkind character sketch." Would you have guessed that the same man painted both? What else differs about the styles?
- Paul Gauguin spoke of wanting to show both sides of himself. He wasn't talking about the two paintings each showing a side, but rather, about each painting showing both sides of himself - essentially the good side and the evil side. Do you see anything in the paintings that reveals this?
- Describe the mood of each portrait.
- Describe the attitude of each version of Gauguin. What might he be like? Are there similarities between the two? What are the differences?
- How are the colors the same? How are they different? What do the colors he used represent to you? Gauguin was very con-cerned with symbolism when he painted; so his color choices were intentional. He wanted you to feel something.
- In the first painting he is holding a paintbrush and palette. In the second he is surrounded by symbols. There is a snake wrapped around his fingers and an apple above his head (sym-bols from the Biblical Garden of Eden). He is surrounded by plants and square, yellow flowers with blue stems. He is wear-ing a halo. What ideas do you think he was trying to commu-nicate?

Camille Pissarro was one of the most import-ant painters in Paris at this time. He became a father figure of not only the Impressionist paint-ers, but also of the four major Post-Impression-ists - Van Gogh, Seurat, Cézanne, and Gauguin. He never created art as eccentric or colorful as the other painters of his day though. His was more dignified, quiet, and sincere. He tried many styles, but always seemed to go back to sim-ple pictures of peasants working and living hum-bly. That, in itself, was quite revolutionary since the people that bought his art were the wealthy.

Additional Layer

It is interesting that Rousseau was so fascinated by the jungle although he never traveled to one to see it firsthand.

Here are a few more of his jungle paintings.

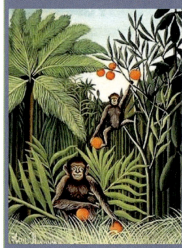

☺ ☻ EXPLORATION: Henri Rousseau's Jungle

Henri Rousseau was inspired by visits to zoos, books, stories, botanical gardens, and pictures of wild animals from magazines. He painted many colorful jungle scenes. His style is called Primitivism, which just means unsophisticated and childlike. Typically primitive artwork is created by untrained artists, but professional artists also use the style if they want to communicate childlike simplicity. In primitive art the perspective, depth, shadows, and proportions often seem a bit off.

Can you see anything that doesn't seem quite lifelike and realistic about this painting?

The Repast Of The Lion by Henri Rousseau

Rousseau also painted close up views of animals peeking out of the jungle. Choose a jungle animal to draw in your sketchbook that will mostly fill up your page. Draw its head. Color it in completely with bright, vivid colors using markers. Now tear pieces of light and dark green tissue paper to adhere around the outside of your page, creating jungle leaves. It should look as though your animal is peeking out of the jungle.

☺ ☺ ☺ EXPLORATION: Henri de Toulouse-Lautrec

Henri de Toulouse-Lautrec liked to paint Paris nightlife. He painted and drew many things, including advertisement posters for the Moulin Rouge, cabaret singers, and businesses with simple line drawings. He is known as the pioneer of modern posters.

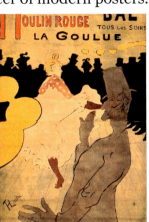

Design a poster for your favorite entertainment spot. It could be a park, a bowling alley or arcade, a movie theater or shopping mall, an amusement park, or a restaurant.

☺ ☺ ☺ EXPLORATION: Dot to Dot With Seurat

Pointillism became popular during this time. Pointillism is forming pictures using tiny dots of paint. When you look at the paintings close up you see lots of colorful dots, but when you stand back, all of the colorful dots blend into a picture.

Visual color mixing occurs, and that is the best part about pointillism. Something that is green can actually be made up of a variety of shades of blue and yellow dots. Our eyes mix the two colors, and we see green.

Seurat made a beautiful pointilism painting of a hot air balloon. Use the hot air balloon printable and create your own hot air

Writer's Workshop

Older students can compare the work of the Post-Impressionists with the art of another era. Look at painting elements and techniques, subject matter, mediums, and themes.

Choose two quintessential pieces, one from each era, and write a compare and contrast essay about them.

Writer's Workshop

Choose a painting from this unit and write a detailed visual description of it. You could do some research on its background and include that as well.

Starry Night's colors are rich and deep. The bright swirling spirals in the sky make the quiet town below almost disappear. The spiky, dark cyprus tree feels gloomy and rough, filling much of the space, but not really drawing the focus in the painting. . .

Famous Folks

Félix Fénéon actively fought against the French government and was even arrested in connection with the assassination of the French president, though he was acquitted.

It took a lot of convincing, but Signac convinced Fénéon to let him paint his portrait. Fénéon said yes, as long as Signac created an effigy, or crude mask-like representation, of his face. Effigies were typically made very quickly with the intent to be destroyed in protest, which is exactly the kind of thing Fénéon would have done.

Instead, Signac painted this colorful profile you see to the right, which became a symbol for the anarchist movement of the day. It shows Fénéon's wit and energetic personality.

balloon pointilism artwork. You can use a cotton swab, the back side of a paintbrush, a toothpick or wooden skewer, or just a tiny brush.

As you paint, use only little dots to fill in the picture. Don't use any sideways motions. Paint as though you are dotting an i over and over again.

☺ ☺ EXPLORATION: Paul and Félix

Paul Signac was an experimenter. He painted all sorts of things in all sorts of ways. He worked with lots of different artists, including Seurat, Van Gogh, and Monet. He tried out their techniques and styles and was always evolving to the next idea. He experimented with a variety of media as well, creating oil paintings, watercolors, pen and ink drawings, etchings, and lithographs.

Most people call this the "Portrait of Félix Fénéon," but the actual name is "Opus 217, Against the Enamel of a Background Rhythmic With Beats and Angles, Tones, and Tints, Portrait of M. Félix Fénéon in 1890." The long title was Signac mocking lengthy scientific terms.

Signac also experimented with ideas. He became an anarchist, rebelling against government and authority. His friend, Félix

Fénéon, was also an anarchist and an art critic and promoter. Signac painted this profile portrait of him using pointilism and an abstraction of the color wheel in the background that looks like a kaleidoscope.

Make your own colorful picture of Félix Fénéon using the printable. In the background swirls, create your own brightly colored and patterned kaleidoscope design.

☺ ☻ EXPLORATION: Auguste Rodin

Auguste Rodin (pronounced row-dan) was the most famous sculptor of the Post-Impressionist era and has become the father of modern sculpture. He spent much of his life working on "The Gates of Hell", a door he sculpted for an art museum in Paris that was never built.

Watch this video about him and his work, but be aware that it shows non-detailed nudes. https://youtu.be/bfv9T1lSO2U

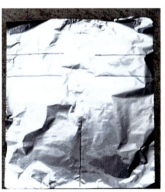 

Use foil to make your own bendable sculpture.

Take a rectangle of foil and divide it into sections as shown, cutting along each line with scissors.

Crumple each section to create a head, arms, and legs. Manipulate the foil into different positions and poses. You can make bends at the knees, elbows, waist, and neck.

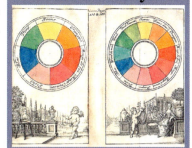
In the late 1800s the color wheel became a topic of scientific discussion. The wheel itself was not new, but scientists were discussing the effects different colors have on people. One of these was an optical theorist by the name of Charles Henry. He and Paul Signac knew each other, and Signac made the illustration of the color wheel on Henry's optical theory about the psychology of visual perception. The new scientific ideas about color influenced the painters of the day.

Coming up next . . .

Unit 4-8

**World War I
Plains States
Earthquakes
Expressionism**

My ideas for this unit:

Title: _____ **Topic:** _____

_____
_____
_____
_____
_____
_____
_____
_____
_____
_____

Title: _____ **Topic:** _____

_____
_____
_____
_____
_____
_____
_____
_____
_____
_____
_____
_____

Title: _____ **Topic:** _____

_____
_____
_____
_____
_____
_____
_____
_____
_____
_____
_____
_____

Title: _____ **Topic:** _____

_____
_____
_____
_____
_____
_____
_____
_____
_____
_____

Title: _____ **Topic:** _____

_____
_____
_____
_____
_____
_____
_____
_____
_____
_____

Title: _____ **Topic:** _____

_____
_____
_____
_____
_____
_____
_____
_____
_____
_____

Civil War Soldier

This is a Civil War soldier who fights for the Union. He is cleaning his gun and checking to be sure it is in good working order. He sits next to his canvas tent, where he will live for months at a time. Most of his life is filled with drills, cleaning equipment, sitting around, and marching to and fro. Occasionally he will fight in a hair raising battle with bullets flying and cannon smashing all around.

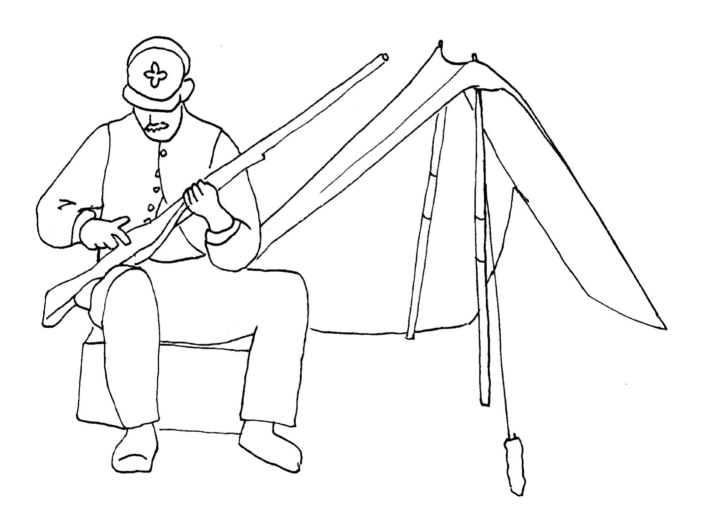

Civil War Timeline

### 1820 Missouri Compromise admits one free state for every slave state. 	### 1850 Compromise of 1850 makes the new territory of California a free state, and allows all other new states and territories to decide for themselves. 	### 1850 Fugitive Slave Act makes it a crime to aid and abet runway slaves, free blacks are kidnapped and carried south as well. 	### 1857 Supreme Court rules against Dred Scott who sues for his freedom; he was ruled to be "property." 
### Oct 1859 John Brown attempts to start a slave revolt by attacking the Federal arsenal at Harper's Ferry, Virginia. 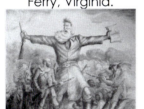	### Nov 1860 Abraham Lincoln elected president 	### Jan 1861 The South secedes 	### April 1861 Attack on Fort Sumter 
### July 1861 First Battle of Bull Run 	### May 1862 "Stonewall" Jackson defeats the North at Shenandoah Valley, almost making it to Washington D.C. 	### Jan 1863 Emancipation Proclamation goes into effect 	### May 1863 Vicksburg Campaign by U.S. Grant, Union win 
### June-July 1863 Battle of Gettysburg 	### Feb 1865 Sherman's March 	### April 1865 Surrender at Appomattox Courthouse 	### April 1865 Lincoln is Assassinated 

Underground Railroad Figures

Layers of Learning

United States 1861

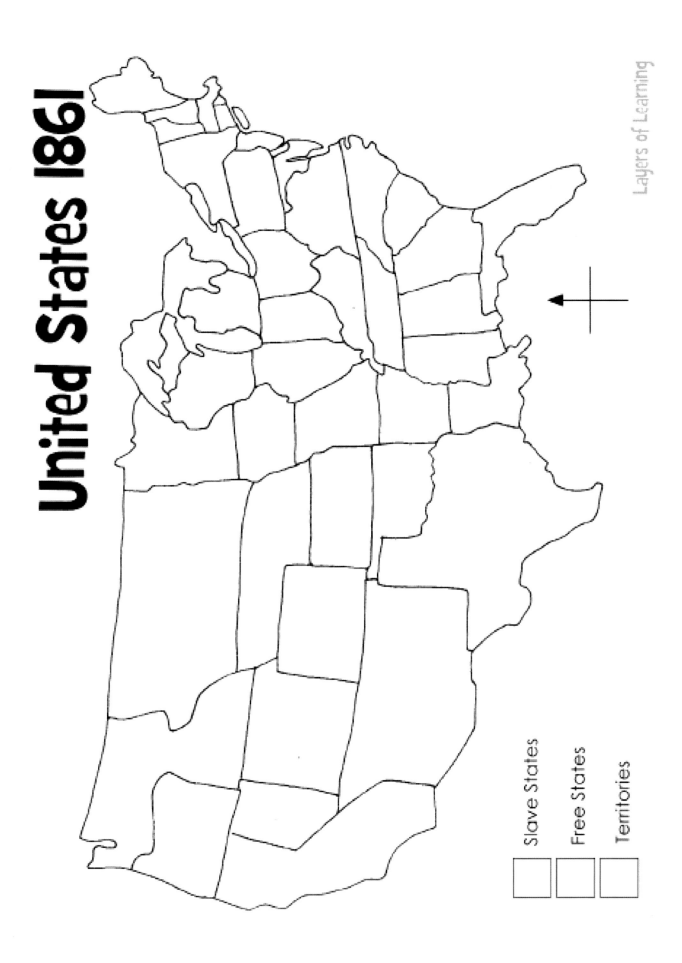

Slave States ☐

Free States ☐

Territories ☐

The powers not delegated to the United States by the Constitution, nor prohibited by it to the States are reserved to the States respectively, or to the people.

Civil War Battles
April 1861 - April 1865

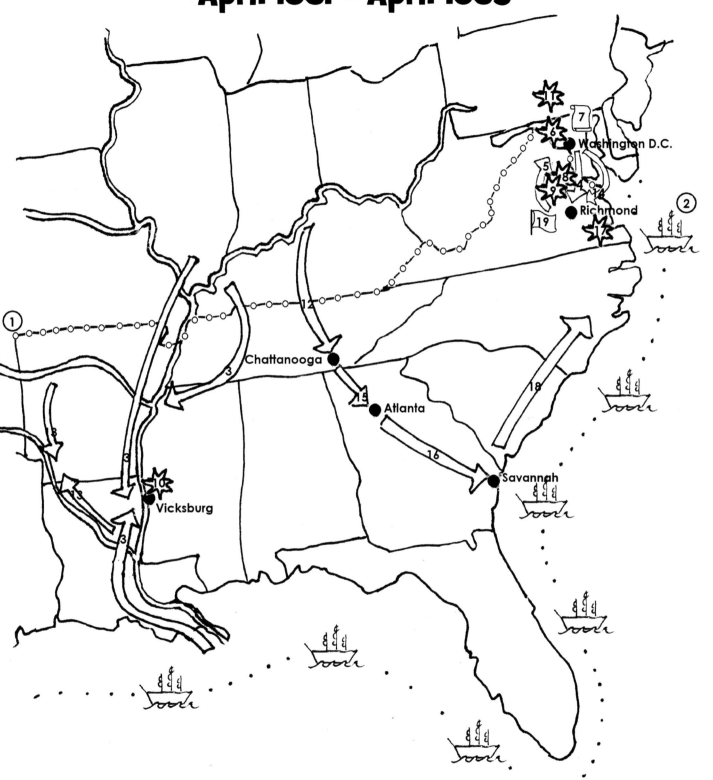

Reconstruction

Carpetbagger	Scalawag
13th Amendment	Freedmen's Bureau
14th Amendment	Sharecropping
15th Amendment	Black Codes and Jim Crow

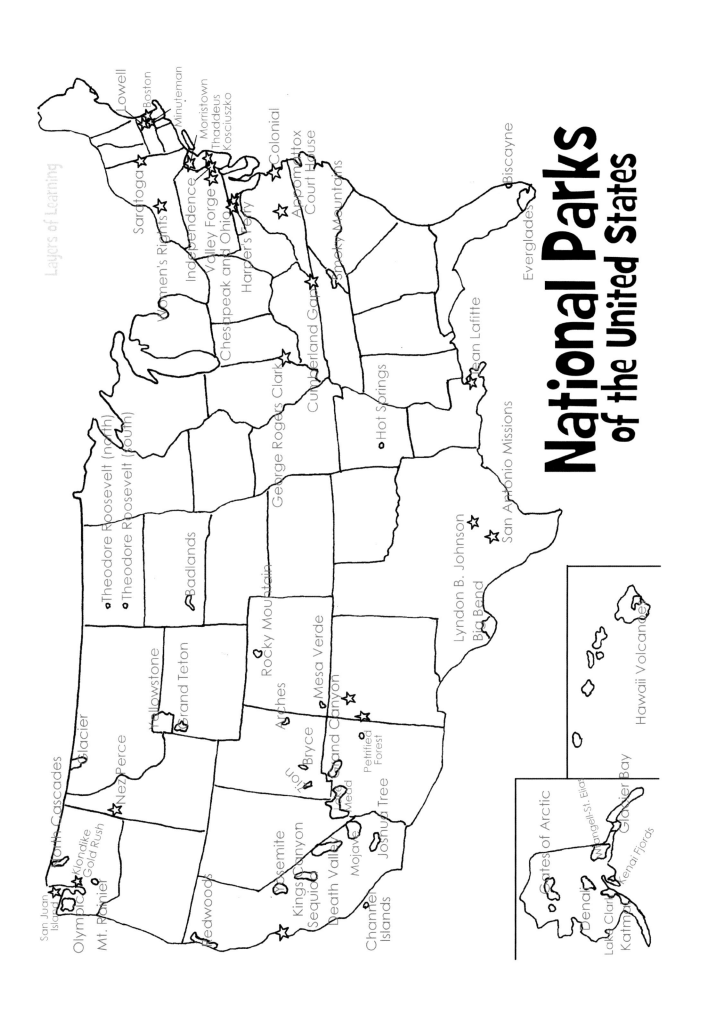

National Parks
of the United States

National Parks Landmarks

Old Faithful

Half Dome

General Sherman Tree

Kilauea Volcano

Carlsbad Caverns

Plate Boundaries

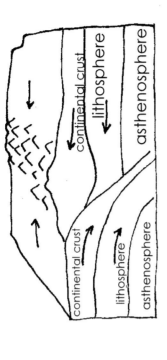

continental collision

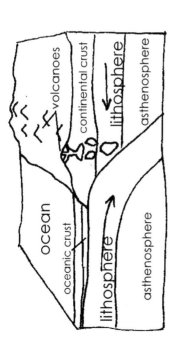

volcanoes

ocean

oceanic crust

subduction

Convergent

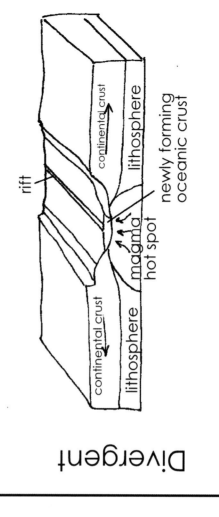

rift

continental crust

lithosphere

newly forming
oceanic crust

magma
hot spot

continental crust

lithosphere

Divergent

oceanic or
continental
crust

Transform Fault

Major Earthquakes Along the Western Coast of South America

Negative numbers indicate south for latitude and west for longitude. Magnitude is not used in the activity but is given for interest. Quakes under 4.0 are not given on the chart.

Latitude	Longitude	Depth	Magnitude
-6.49	-80.26	41	4.3
-28.63	-69.28	83	4.5
-15.02	-70.87	22	4.5
-5.8	-76.88	27	4.3
-15.05	-70.69	74	4.7
-5.76	-80.85	37	4.6
-34.87	-74.04	14	4.6
-14.17	-75.64	43	6.4
-0.13	-78.37	3	4
-14.44	-75.97	24	6.9
-1.27	-77.31	207	7.1
-0.96	-77.82	35	5.4
-11.78	-75.63	10	4.6
-10.37	-75.51	33	5.5
-12.18	-77.16	51	5.3
-2.31	-77.84	123	6.8
-13.37	-76.6	39	8
-3.99	-79.84	50	4.5
-13.46	-76.63	23	6.7
-5.8	-78.7	40	5.4
-0.51	-77.75	35	4.8
-5.68	-76.4	115	7.5
-1.36	-80.79	17	6.1
-0.59	-80.39	33	7.2
-14.99	-75.68	33	7.7
-1.04	-78.74	33	5.9
-9.59	-79.59	10	7.5

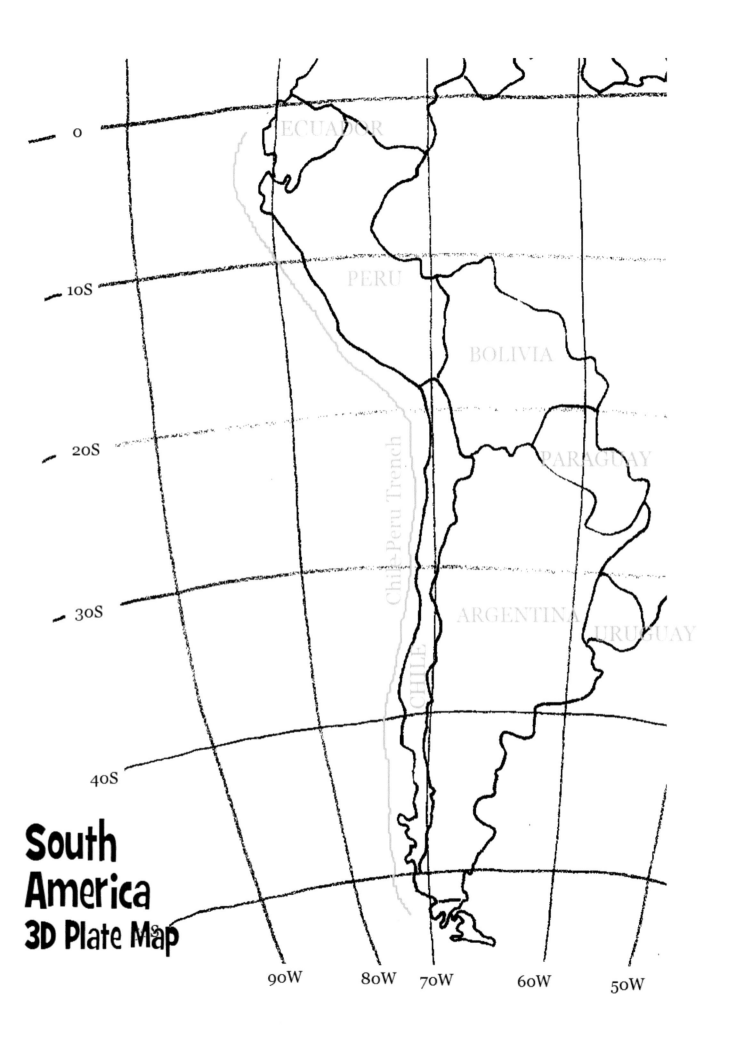

ECUADOR

PERU

BOLIVIA

PARAGUAY

Chile-Peru Trench

ARGENTINA

URUGUAY

CHILE

0

10S

20S

30S

40S

90W   80W   70W   60W   50W

**South
America
3D Plate Map**

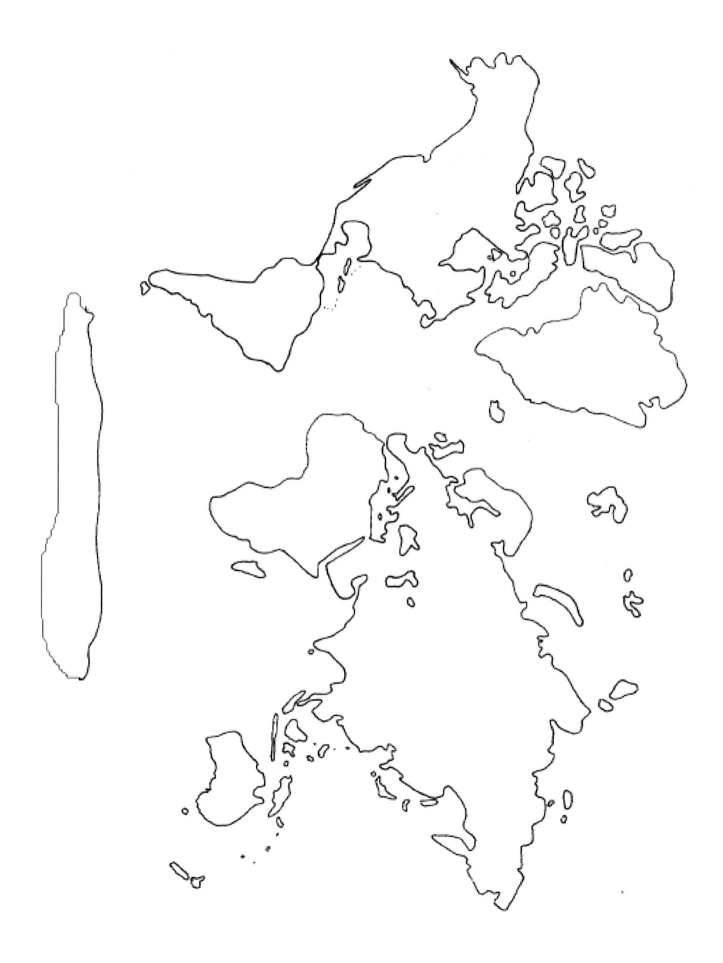

Ring of Fire Notes

Name: _____

Date: _____

What and where is the Ring of Fire?

Volcanoes of the Ring of Fire

What is subduction, and what is the evidence for it?

Summary

Ring of Fire Quiz

Name: _____

Date: _____

1. Where is the Ring of Fire located?

2. Contrast the lava found in Hawaii with the lava of the Ring of Fire.

3. What are the two types of lava called, and which is more dangerous?

4. What is a subduction zone? Include a labeled drawing in your answer.

5. Give at least one piece of evidence scientists have found that the Ring of Fire is created by subduction zones?

About the Authors

Karen & Michelle . . .
Mothers, sisters, teachers, women who are passionate
about educating kids.
We are dedicated to lifelong learning.

Karen, a mother of four, who has homeschooled her kids for more than eight years with her husband, Bob, has a bachelor's degree in child development with an emphasis in education. She lives in Idaho, gardens, teaches piano, and plays an excruciating number of board games with her kids. Karen is our resident arts expert and English guru {most necessary as Michelle regularly and carelessly mangles the English language and occasionally steps over the bounds of polite society}.

Michelle and her husband, Cameron, have homeschooled their six boys for more than a decade. Michelle earned a bachelors in biology, making her the resident science expert, though she is mocked by her friends for being the Botanist with the Black Thumb of Death. She also is the go-to for history and government. She believes in staying up late, hot chocolate, and a no whining policy. We both pitch in on geography, in case you were wondering.

Visit our constantly updated blog for tons of free ideas,
free printables, and more cool stuff for sale:
www.Layers-of-Learning.com

Made in the USA
Middletown, DE
04 April 2025